The Essentials of
MANAGING
CHANGE *and*
TRANSITION

The Business Literacy for HR Professionals Series

The Business Literacy for HR Professionals Series educates human resource professionals in the principles, practices, and processes of business and management. Developed in conjunction with the Society for Human Resource Management, these books provide a comprehensive overview of the concepts, skills, and tools HR professionals need to be influential partners in developing and executing organizational strategy. Drawing on rich content from Harvard Business School Publishing and the Society for Human Resource Management, each volume is closely reviewed by a content expert as well as by senior HR professionals. Whether you are aspiring to the executive level in your organization or already in a leadership position, these authoritative books provide the basic business knowledge you need to play a strategic role.

Other books in the series:

The Essentials of Finance and Budgeting
The Essentials of Negotiation

BUSINESS LITERACY FOR HR PROFESSIONALS

The Essentials of
MANAGING
CHANGE *and*
TRANSITION

Harvard Business School Press
Boston, Massachusetts

and
Society for Human Resource Management
Alexandria, Virginia

Library of Congress Cataloging-in-Publication Data

Business literacy for HR professionals: the essentials of managing change and
transition.
    p.   cm. — (The business literacy for HR professionals series)
Includes bibliographical references and index.
ISBN 1-59139-573-9 (pbk.: alk. paper)
    1. Personnel management. 2. Organizational change. 3. Organizational
effectiveness. I. Title: Essentials of managing change and transition. II. Series.
HF5549.H343 2005
658.3'01—dc22

                                                                    2004014043

Contents

Introduction   *xiii*

1 The Ever-Changing Workplace   1
Understanding HR's Role in Organizational Change

    The Forces of Change   2
    New Capabilities for Organizations   4
    A Strategic Approach to Change Management   5
    HR's Dual Role in Organizational Change   10
    Summing Up   11
    Leveraging Chapter Insights: Critical Questions   18

2 Dimensions of Change   21
Examining Types and Approaches

    Types of Change Programs   22
    Three Tactics for Timing Change   24
    Two Different Approaches to Change   26
    Summing Up   31
    Leveraging Chapter Insights: Critical Questions   34

3 Is Your Organization Change-Ready?   35
Preparing for Companywide Change

    Respected and Effective Leaders   36
    Appropriate Reward Systems   39
    A Nonhierarchical Organization   41
    Shaping a Change-Ready Organization   42
    Summing Up   47
    Leveraging Chapter Insights: Critical Questions   47

4   Are You and Your Employees Change-Ready?   49
    Preparing for Individual Change

    Characteristics of Change-Ready Individuals   50
    The Importance of Motivation   51
    HR Professionals: Key Motivational Players   57
    Summing Up   66
    Leveraging Chapter Insights: Critical Questions   66

5   Eight Steps to Change   69
    A Systematic Approach

    The Eight Steps   71
    Step 1: Establish a Sense of Urgency   71
    Step 2: Create a Guiding Coalition   76
    Step 3: Develop a Compelling Vision   76
    Step 4: Communicate the Vision   78
    Step 5: Empower Others to Act on the Vision   79
    Step 6: Generate Short-Term Wins   80
    Step 7: Consolidate Gains and Produce More Change 81
    Step 8: Anchor New Approaches in the Company's Culture   81
    Leaders and Managers: Roles for HR Professionals   83
    Summing Up   87
    Leveraging Chapter Insights: Critical Questions   87

6   Implementation   91
    Putting Your Change Plans in Motion

    Enlist the Support and Involvement of Key People   93
    Craft an Implementation Plan   94
    Communicate Relentlessly   97
    Support Your Implementation Plan with Consistent
        Behaviors and Messages   102
    Develop Enabling Structures   104
    Create Results-Driven Change   106
    Celebrate Milestones   107
    Use Consultants Wisely   109
    Summing Up   113
    Leveraging Chapter Insights: Critical Questions   114

7   How Employees Respond to Change   115
    A Continuum of Styles

        Common Responses to Change   116
        The Resisters   120
        The Change Agents   124
        Summing Up   126
        Leveraging Chapter Insights: Critical Questions   129

8   Helping Employees Adapt to Change   131
    Strategies to Reduce Stress

        Loss and Anxiety   133
        Reacting to Change: Four Stages   134
        The Conventional Advice   136
        What Individuals Can Do for Themselves   138
        Helping Managers Assist Their Employees During Change   144
        Rethinking Resisters   152
        How HR Professionals Can Cope with Change-Related
            Stress   154
        Summing Up   157
        Leveraging Chapter Insights: Critical Questions   158

9   Toward Continuous Change   159
    Staying Competitive Through Change

        Continuous Incremental Change   161
        Can People Handle It?   162
        HR's Role in Driving Ongoing Change   165
        Summing Up   172
        Leveraging Chapter Insights: Critical Questions   173

10 Common Change-Management Challenges
    for HR Professionals   175
    Handling Them Effectively and Successfully

        Downsizing Initiatives   176
        Companywide Restructurings   184
        Corporate Acquisitions and Mergers   186
        Selection and Assimilation of New Leaders 192

Restructuring of the HR Function   197
New Approaches to Key HR Programs   200
Summing Up   203
Leveraging Chapter Insights: Critical Questions   205

11   HR as Change Agent   207
An Unprecedented Opportunity—and Responsibility

Strategic Partners in Action   208
Where to Go from Here?   211
Checklist for Leading a Successful Change Initiative   216
Summing Up   220
Leveraging Chapter Insights: Critical Questions   221

Appendix A   223
Implementation Tools

Appendix B   231
*Choosing Change-Management Consultants and
Outplacement Firms*

Notes   237
For Further Reading   243
Index   247
About the Series Adviser   257
About the Subject Adviser   259
About the Writers   261
About the Society for Human Resource Management   263
Acknowledgments   265

Introduction

Pick any industry, and chances are that it looks very different now than it did a decade ago. And the companies within that industry have experienced their own unique upheavals. For example, IBM was adrift and slowly sinking before it was rescued and refitted under new leadership and a core of energetic and determined employees. Microsoft transformed itself from a software company to an integrator of computer-Internet solutions. General Electric endured several successive waves of change over the past few decades. And Enron rose like a rocket on its innovative approach to energy trading before overreaching management blew it to bits. These companies represent only a few episodes in the saga of corporate transformation.

Although it's impossible to anticipate the when, what, and where of change, the fact that the business landscape will keep shifting *is* something you and other HR professionals can count on—and should plan for. Why? As an HR executive or manager, you can play a central role in enabling your firm to anticipate, adapt to, and profit from change—especially if you view change not as a threat but as an opportunity to help your company reinvent itself. As one recent study revealed, HR executives today rated the challenge of managing change as the most important HR issue on their minds.[1] As managers of their companies' human assets, HR professionals can play a crucial role in leading *and* facilitating change—as well as building a capacity for ongoing change in their firms.

It all starts with knowing when change is on the horizon. The following developments are near-certain indicators:

- **A merger, acquisition, or divestiture.** Mergers and acquisitions are often the means by which organizations grow. Divestitures are strategic attempts to redirect assets or to focus the organization in some particular direction. Such "restructuring" changes almost always result in duplications of functions, which many firms correct through painful layoffs.

- **The launch of a new product or service.** New offerings connect a company with new customer markets and, often, new competitors. Managers and employees must adapt to and learn from these realities.

- **A new leader.** The arrival of any new leader heralds change. Like a new owner of an old house, an incoming leader will likely want to remodel existing business processes. In many cases, this means a substantial turnover among senior executives. Change cascades further down from these new executives.

- **A new technology.** Technology is transforming the world of work. Information technology in particular is altering not just how we work, but when we work and from which locations. Close to 23 percent of the U.S. workforce now does some amount of "telework" from home, from a client location, or from a satellite office. In addition, so-called "disruptive" technologies can render a company's products or services obsolete in a very short time. Where are all the "supercomputers" we used to hear about? And who needs travelers' checks in an age of credit cards and ATMs? Every day, products that we used to take for granted are being displaced by radical new offerings.

- **An economic upturn or downturn.** When a nation's economy takes an upswing or suffers an overall decline, industries and companies experience—and often initiate—major change. During good times, executives may decide to expand their company's product or service offerings or invest in new capacities. During hard times, many firms institute aggressive cost-cutting measures, such as downsizing or outsourcing. Whether the economic climate is rosy or grim, organizations of all sizes, and in all industries, can count on the need to transform themselves to seize opportunities and remain competitive.

The fact that organizations must undergo continual change doesn't mean that people *enjoy* altering the way they work. On the contrary, many people find change disheartening and frustrating. And most change initiatives leave a number of casualties in their wake. Managers often complain that change takes too long or that it's too costly. Alternately, some worry that it doesn't last long enough or have enough financial backing to get the job done. People at the bottom claim that the "top" doesn't practice what it preaches. Those at the top lament that the folks at the bottom are dragging their feet. People in the middle blame everyone else.

Nevertheless, change is an inescapable part of organizational life, and is essential for progress. Those who know how to anticipate it, catalyze it, and manage it will find their careers more satisfying—and will help sharpen their companies' competitive edge. As change agents, you and other HR professionals can help to identify and implement needed change processes, as well as coach other executives and managers to do the same. You can also assist other managers in helping their employees let go of long-standing cultural characteristics and embrace new ones.

In addition, you have to strike a delicate balance between respecting your organization's tradition and history while acting to enable a better future. As HR management expert and author Dave Ulrich writes, you "may need to force or facilitate a dialogue about values as [you] identify new behaviors that will help to keep [your] firm competitive over time. . . . [All this requires a talent for] identifying and framing problems, building relationships of trust, solving problems, and creating—and fulfilling—action plans."[2]

HR professionals must thus balance the need for change, innovation, and transformation with the need for continuity, discipline, and stability. After all, if a company is too constant and stable, it can't change with the times. But if it's awash in too much change, destructive chaos reigns. To help your organization achieve just the right balance, you need to enable managers and employees to resolve several paradoxes:[3]

- **Past versus future.** Past successes ensure current survival, but only by letting go of aspects of the past can companies move forward into their future.

- **Free agency versus control.** People need autonomy to make decisions, while at the same time their companies require discipline among employees to transform individual efforts into team achievements and to set boundaries around freedom.

- **Efficiency versus innovation.** Companies need to maintain efficiency while also taking the risks that lead to innovation. Thus risks must be bounded rather than haphazard.

To resolve these paradoxes and serve as change agents, HR professionals must master four agendas:[4]

- **Change champion:** publicly supporting transformation efforts defined by the company's top executives

- **Change facilitator:** enabling change by, for example, offering external facilitators technical support as well as insights into the company's political dynamics, history, and culture, or by developing training programs that yield a supply of internal facilitators

- **Change designer:** redesigning HR systems such as staffing, development, performance appraisal, rewards, organization design, and communication practices to help managers and employees understand and feel a sense of ownership over a change initiative

- **Change demonstrator:** manifesting a change initiative within their own function, and serving as a leading example of effective transformation

All of this constitutes a tall order—but this book is designed to help you make the transition.

How to Use This Book

In this book, you'll discover how to manage change constructively, and how to help yourself and others in your company navigate the upheavals of change. You'll also learn practical strategies for making change initiatives more successful and less painful for everyone involved.

The literature on change management is large and growing constantly, with dozens of books and case studies published every year. This book compiles the best information on this subject in a manageable, practical format. It provides essential information on how HR professionals can lead or facilitate change in their organizations. In each chapter, you'll find a wealth of examples from the contemporary business scene, and numerous practical tips to make your efforts more effective.

Chapter 1 examines the accelerating forces of change buffeting businesses today. It then lays out the new role HR can—and must—play in helping their companies adapt and profit from change. That new role requires new capabilities and a strategic approach to change management, which the chapter also explores.

Chapter 2 offers an overview of the types of change programs initiated by organizations. These include structural, cultural, and process change, as well as change that aims strictly to cut costs. The chapter also weighs the pros and cons of anticipating versus reacting to change, and compares two distinctly different approaches to change.

Chapter 3 explores the importance of companywide "change-readiness." It identifies three key characteristics of a change-ready organization—respected and effected leaders, appropriate reward systems, and a nonhierarchical organizational structure—and offers practical advice for strengthening these aspects of your company.

Chapter 4 shifts the focus from organizationwide change-readiness to individual change-readiness, examining the defining characteristics of change-ready people and exploring the role of motivation. You'll find numerous guidelines for enhancing motivation by challenging complacency, giving people a voice in the changes affecting them, and driving out the fear often associated with change.

Chapter 5 details eight steps that can boost your chances of launching and implementing a successful change initiative. You'll discover effective and not-so-effective actions to take during change efforts, and find a helpful list of mistakes to avoid.

Chapter 6 turns to implementation—the toughest part of change management. This chapter is organized around key implementation activities: mobilizing support, planning the initiative, encouraging behaviors that are consistent with the plan, building enabling structures, focusing people on results, celebrating milestones, and communicating about the change initiative relentlessly.

Chapter 7 delves into the range of responses people have to change. The managers and employees who populate organizational systems have identities, relationships, and emotions that change almost always destabilizes. As an HR professional, you must recognize the power of the social systems in which change unfolds. To that end, the chapter focuses on resisters (and how to deal with them) and change agents (and how to leverage their energy).

Chapter 8 takes a closer look at the feelings of loss and anxiety associated with change, and offers guidelines for easing your own and others' stress during times of change. When we're forced to undergo change, we often go through a "mourning" process characterized by an initial period of shock, followed by defensive retreat, then acknowledgment, and finally acceptance and adaptation. The more you can help yourself and others throughout your organization to navigate through this process, the more effectively you'll manage change.

Chapter 9 addresses the topic of continuous change, raising questions such as: Is it possible? Can managers and employees handle it? Will too much change create more problems than it solves? This chapter answers these questions and provides practical advice on how to sculpt your organization, via small, manageable steps, into one that is always changing and improving.

Chapter 10 focuses on the change-management challenges that place unique burdens on HR. These include companywide restructurings, downsizing initiatives, corporate acquisitions and mergers, selection and assimilation of new leaders, restructuring of the HR function, and new approaches to HR programs such as compensation, benefits, performance appraisal, and so forth. You'll see examples of how HR professionals in other firms have handled each of these challenges and find practical "do's and don'ts" for each situation.

Chapter 11, finally, steps back and reviews the opportunity—and responsibility—for HR professionals to play a strategic role as change agents in their organizations. It describes the behaviors that characterize strategic partners and lays out a three-phase process for taking on this role. The chapter concludes with a checklist for leading a successful change initiative in your firm.

Two appendices supplement the chapters. The first of these offers worksheets and checklists you can use in managing different aspects of organizational change. The second is a primer on how to hire and use change-management consultants and select outplacement firms.

Although the materials in this book won't make you an expert on change management, they do provide authoritative, *essential* advice you can use to get going and to stay on track. If you want to learn more, see the reading list included at the back of the book.

The content in this book is based on books, articles, and online products of the Society for Human Resource Management (SHRM) and Harvard Business School Publishing. SHRM resources include numerous white papers and surveys from SHRM's Web site, articles from *HR Magazine,* and books published or copublished by SHRM. Harvard Business School Publishing resources include class notes prepared by Todd Jick on implementation and the problems people experience in adapting to change; the change management modules in Harvard ManageMentor®, an online service; and change management books and articles authored by Dave Ulrich, Michael Beer, Bert Spector, Russell Eisenstat, Nitin Nohria, John Kotter, and other leading thinkers.

For additional resources, visit the SHRM Web site at www.SHRM. org and the HBSP Web site at www.harvardbusinessonline.com.

The Essentials of

MANAGING
CHANGE *and*
TRANSITION

CHAPTER ONE

The Ever-Changing Workplace

*Understanding HR's Role
in Organizational Change*

Key Topics Covered in This Chapter

* *An overview of changes affecting today's workplace*

* *New capabilities companies need to compete in the face of change*

* *The importance of change-management skills for HR professionals*

* *HR's dual role in change management*

C HANGE has always been a fact of life in the world of work—but this is truer today than ever. As the new millennium dawns, the winds of change are buffeting business from every direction—and with hurricane speed. To help their organizations stay competitive in the face of ever-accelerating shifts in business life, HR professionals first need to understand the forces of change. Then they must use that understanding to help their companies build the specific capabilities needed to anticipate, adapt to, and leverage change so as to remain competitive.

The Forces of Change

Business change stems from several major sources. Here's a sampling:[1]

- **A company's success or failure.** Whether an organization enjoys spectacular growth and profitability or suffers difficulty or even failure, change will often result. In the case of business success, a company's leaders may decide to invest profits in new product-development or marketing efforts or make some other changes in the way it does business. In the case of business difficulty or failure, leaders may overhaul processes or launch other efforts to turn the business around.

- **Environmental factors.** These include *regulatory changes* (such as deregulation across the utility, telecommunications, transportation, and energy industries) and *technological innovation* (for example, speedier information processing, data access, communication, and transfer of goods, capital, and knowledge).

- **Business trends.** One such trend is *globalization*—the spreading of commercial activity internationally. Globalization stiffens *competition* among companies seeking to do business in new markets and cultures.

- **Stakeholder expectations.** These comprise *employees'* growing demand to have challenging, rewarding work, as well as *consumers* who expect companies to protect the environment and improve the communities in which they do business. In addition, *customers* want ever more affordable and high-quality products and services. And *shareholders*—particularly baby boomers nearing retirement—demand increasingly impressive short-term financial returns on their investments in companies.

- **Demographic shifts.** For some nations, these include *aging populations*—which can mean a shrinking labor pool and rising health-care costs. Demographic shifts may also take the form of increasing *ethnic diversity*, a rise in the number of *foreign-born workers,* and greater *variety in family structure.* With these kinds of changes, companies must pay special attention to matters of discrimination, civil rights, and employment law.

- **Social, economic, and political changes.** These consist of events and developments—such as *terrorist attacks, economic downturns,* and *global political conflicts*—that force companies to focus on safety and security.

Clearly, change can take many forms and can come at a company from just about any direction. Moreover, change affects all companies, in every industry. What must organizations do to survive *and* thrive in the face of change? They have to develop new capabilities that enable them to respond to change—and even profit from it.

New Capabilities for Organizations

As change accelerates, organizations in every industry need to cultivate a broad range of capabilities not only to survive but also to stay ahead of rivals. That means developing the ability to:

- Deliver higher-quality products and services faster and at lower costs than competitors

- Strengthen company brands—consumers' perceptions of what a company does best

- Identify and take advantage of synergies that arise from teamwork within an organization as well as alliances and partnerships a company forges with other organizations

- Constantly renew company offerings through innovation and fresh thinking

To remain successful in the face of unrelenting change, firms also need to remake their organizational structures, systems, and cultures. Table 1-1 shows some examples.

TABLE 1-1

The New Organization

Rather than . . .	Companies will need to . . .
Being structured bureaucratically, with multiple hierarchical levels . . .	Become less bureaucratic, have fewer rules and hierarchical levels, and let lower-level employees take on more managerial responsibilities
Distributing performance information and offering management training and support systems only to senior managers and executives . . .	Provide performance information, as well as management training and support systems, to a broader range of employees
Establishing a culture of avoiding risk, looking inward, making decisions slowly, and being centralized . . .	Tolerate more risk, look outward, make decisions quickly, and distribute power beyond just the topmost level

Source: Adapted from John P. Kotter, *Leading Change* (Boston: Harvard Business School Press, 1996), 172.

If all this strikes you as overly daunting, take a deep breath and consider what it might really be like to work for an organization that can anticipate, adapt to, and benefit from change. As John Kotter notes in his book *Leading Change*:

> *Truly adaptive firms . . . are awesome competitive machines. They produce superb products and services faster and better. They run circles around bloated bureaucracies. Even when they have far fewer resources and patents or less market share, they compete and win again and again. . . . Living and winning in that environment can be fun, because you feel like you're doing something worthwhile. . . . It's challenging. It's never boring. . . . And for most of us, making a real contribution is pleasing to the soul.[2]*

Though Kotter's description sounds enticing, building a change-adaptive organization takes commitment, courage, and careful attention to every aspect of how a company operates. HR professionals can—indeed, they must—play a central role in the building process. How? They need to take a strategic approach to change management.

A Strategic Approach to Change Management

By managing change, HR professionals can help their organizations compete despite shifts in the business landscape. But to do so, they must cultivate a broad range of competencies—ranging from managing a company's culture to engaging in business and strategy planning. Together, these competencies enable HR to take a strategic approach to change. Let's take a closer look at the competencies below.[3]

Culture Management

When HR professionals manage their company's culture, they influence shared ways of thinking and behaving across the organization. In the most change-adaptive organizations, these men and women understand what kind of culture the company needs to support its business strategy as well as satisfy customers and employees.

In addition, HR professionals at successful firms translate the desired culture into clearly defined, specific behaviors and attitudes. For example, in a company that needs a culture marked by creative thinking, a tolerance for mistakes and a willingness to share knowledge would likely count among the most essential behaviors and attitudes.

Change Acceleration

In addition to shaping their organizations' culture, HR professionals seeking to build change-adaptive companies must seek ways to accelerate change throughout their firm. They can do this in several ways:

- Adapting what they've learned about change to new change initiatives

- Monitoring progress of change processes

- Encouraging themselves and others throughout the organization to make change happen quickly

- Analyzing what it is that permits some decisions to be made quickly, then applying their insights to the decision-making process

- Ensuring the availability of resources (such as money, information, and people) needed to catalyze change

Strategic Decision Making

As another change-management competency, HR professionals need to enable strategic decision making in their companies. They can do this by playing two roles:

- **Proactive.** They understand the business enough to set the direction of change, form opinions about the company's future, and present well-informed arguments on strategic issues.

- **Reactive.** They respond to others' ideas by playing "devil's advocate"—asking provocative, insightful questions and anticipating barriers to implementing the company's strategy.

Market Understanding

To take a strategic approach to change, HR professionals also have to develop a keen understanding of the organization's market, as well as know how to enable others within the organization to acquire the same understanding. The key? Being able to gather and disseminate vital information generated from the business environment.

For instance, in some firms, HR managers have initiated employee orientation programs in which newly recruited workers spend time in consumers' homes to observe how customers shop for and use various products. In other companies, HR programs have encouraged managers and employees to conduct market research, either face-to-face or over the phone, to gather accurate feedback about how the company's products or services are perceived in the marketplace.

Business and Strategic Planning

Finally, HR professionals must be savvy business and strategic planners themselves if they hope to help their organizations adapt to change. Business planning and strategic planning are two different things—and HR executives and managers need to understand the distinction.[4]

- **Business planning.** A business plan lays out a company's specific operational goals and provides the basis for budgeting and forecasting. Typically, the plan covers a shorter time horizon and a narrower range of subject matter than a strategic plan does. Business plans also contain performance indicators with which managers can measure progress on plan goals.

In most companies, each major business unit—including the HR unit—creates a business plan for each budget cycle. Every business plan contains a section on allocation of resources—including human resources. HR managers need to identify the human resource contribution needed for each unit to achieve the objectives in its plan.

- **Strategic planning.** A strategic plan documents executives' thinking about how their company will compete successfully under uncertain conditions—that is, how it will distinguish itself from its rivals and offer customers unique value that no other competitor can provide.

  HR can play a vital role in strategic planning by understanding four crucial aspects of strategy: (1) *strategic intent,* including what the company is trying to accomplish and how it plans to add value in the marketplace; (2) *future scenarios,* or what shape the company's future might take, given current realities; (3) *strategic positioning,* or how the company plans to deal with the various future scenarios executives have defined; and (4) *human resource issues,* or whether the organization's workforce has the skills, systems, and processes needed to secure its strategic position.

  HR professionals can contribute to strategic planning by encouraging executives to explore the business implications of the firm's strategic intent and future scenarios, and shaping the firm's human capital to put the company in the best position possible to compete. HR professionals may also be called upon to facilitate strategic planning meetings or to find qualified consultants to do so.

See "HR in Action: Leading Change After September 11, 2001" to learn how HR professionals drove change on all these fronts to turn around one company in crisis.

HR in Action: Leading Change After September 11, 2001

Terry Kassel had to hit the ground running when she started her job as executive vice president of human resources at Merrill Lynch on September 22, 2001. With the economy stumbling, terrorists attacking, and securities authorities examining the company's ethics, Merrill Lynch faced its biggest challenges ever.

First, to help the company regain its footing, Kassel soon became an accomplished change agent. She began by identifying an overcapacity of people and bloated cost structure— symptoms that had begun plaguing much of Wall Street during boom times. Then she changed systems, processes, and technologies to support the company's newly formulated strategy of becoming "a new kind of financial services firm—a growth company with a culture that is diversified and disciplined, agile and accountable."

Kassel established a company-run HR call center, which employees could access any time to get their questions answered quickly and accurately. Then she applied "a strong dose of Web-based technology in the form of employee and manager self-service via the company intranet, combined with call centers."

Kassel also directed her unit to work closely with Merrill Lynch's CEO and his direct reports to set up a talent-assessment process that supported the company's diversification efforts. These efforts comprised building new client relationships with a range of communities, as well as recruiting minority, female, and disabled employees.

Finally, Kassel's group coordinates the dissemination of all information regarding change initiatives at Merrill Lynch. The goal? To ensure that employees throughout the organization understand how the company's competitive environment has

Continued

shifted and why the firm must make specific changes to survive. Town hall meetings, communications through the company's intranet, and companywide e-mails all ensure that information remains timely, responsive, and proactive.

Kassel's activities as change agent have paid big dividends. Despite all the turbulence of 2001–2003, "there haven't been any mass defections," she says. "Morale was never an issue." Aligning HR's efforts behind business strategy has generated impressive financial results as well: Merrill Lynch's operating earnings rose from $2.4 billion in 2001 to $2.6 billion in 2002—despite a brutal economic downturn. And its fourth-quarter net operating earnings jumped from $491 million in 2001 to $615 million a year later.

SOURCE: "Surviving the Storm." *Human Resource Executive,* August 2003.

HR's Dual Role in Organizational Change

In taking a strategic approach to change management, HR professionals can apply the above competencies while serving in several roles:

- **Change agents** initiate and lead the organizational changes that a company must make to remain competitive in the face of major business shifts

- **Change facilitators** support change initiatives launched by others in the organization.

Each of these roles generates crucial value in an organization, and an HR executive or manager might find him- or herself alternating between the two, depending on circumstances. What do HR-professionals-turned-change-agents-and-facilitators look like in action? According to consultant and author Cris Hagen, you can think of them as the following:[5]

- **"Scouts"** scan the external and internal business landscape to identify their company's strengths and weaknesses related to people, processes, structures, and technologies; assess potential threats and the company's ability to overcome those threats; and spot opportunities to improve operations and put the right talent in place to support the company's business strategy.

- **"Chess masters"** identify and coach individuals who can best lead change efforts; develop and communicate key messages supporting change champions; and deploy human resources to best influence the outcome of a change initiatives.

- **"Cartographers"** provide a "road map" describing the steps, tools, and techniques necessary for the company to navigate major change, including how the company will address barriers to a change initiative.

- **"Architects"** rethink the design of systems and processes for managing human performance, such as job-classification systems, compensation and incentive systems, training and development programs, and informal recognition systems.

Use assessment tool 1-1 to gauge your abilities as a change agent.

When you've completed this tool, see assessment tool 1-2, which helps you evaluate your current understanding of the concepts you'll encounter in later chapters in this book.

Summing Up

In this chapter, you learned about the forces of change—including environmental factors; business trends; shifting stakeholder expectations; and demographic, social, political, and economic changes.

You also discovered the new capabilities companies today must strengthen in order to remain competitive in the face of constant change. These include:

- Delivering higher-quality products and services faster and at lower costs than competitors

- Strengthening company brands

Assessment Tool 1-1
Rate Your Change-Agent Skills

For each statement below, circle the number that best describes how true it is with regard to what you do as an HR professional. "1" indicates "not at all true"; "5" indicates "very true."

1. I help my organization adapt to change.

    1   2   3   4   5

2. I shape culture change for renewal and transformation in my organization.

    1   2   3   4   5

3. I initiate processes and programs designed to increase my organization's ability to change.

    1   2   3   4   5

4. I help my organization anticipate and adapt to issues that will be a concern in the future.

    1   2   3   4   5

5. I am perceived as a change agent in my organization.

    1   2   3   4   5

6. I actively support new behaviors that will enable my organization to remain competitive.

    1   2   3   4   5

7. I participate personally in renewal, change, and transformation in my organization.

    1   2   3   4   5

8. I reshape behavior in ways that enable organizational change.

    1   2   3   4   5

9. I develop processes and programs to help my organization transform itself.

    1   2   3   4   5

10. My credibility in the organization stems from my ability to make change happen.

    1   2   3   4   5

Calculating Your Score

To calculate your score, add up the numbers you circled.

Interpreting Your Score

The higher your score, the greater your skill as a change agent.

Score 38-50: You have a solid mastery of the skills an HR professional needs to serve as a change agent. You encourage change ready behaviors in others and practice them yourself, as well as take active steps to enable your organization to implement positive change.

Score 24-37: You have some understanding of the skills an HR professional needs to serve as a change agent. However, you could do more to strengthen your skills.

Score 10-23: You would benefit from deepening your understanding of the change-agent role for HR professionals, as well as strengthening your skills in this area.

SOURCE: Adapted from Dave Ulrich, *Human Resource Champions: The Next Agenda for Adding Value and Delivering Results.* (Boston: Harvard Business School Press, 1997), 49-50.

Assessment Tool 1-2
Test Your Understanding of HR and Change

To gauge your current understanding of the concepts in this book, take the following multiple-choice test. Then review the answer key that follows, which points you to particular chapters for more information on specific aspects of change.

1. *Most* change programs fall into which of the following categories?
   A. Structural and leadership change
   B. Cost cutting
   C. Process and cultural change
   D. All of the above

2. Which of the following is *most* essential for an organization to be change-ready?
   A. Leaders who have others' respect and who have earned a reputation for effectiveness
   B. Reward systems that provide incentive for preserving business practices that have led to success in the past
   C. A hierarchical managerial structure that accelerates decision making
   D. Pay plans that encourage a positive attitude about change

3. Which of the following is *not* a common characteristic of change-ready individuals?
   A. An ability to make the most of any situation
   B. A calmness in the face of unnerving new experiences
   C. A desire to take risks
   D. A belief that they can handle a difficult situation

4. **What should HR leaders do first to launch a major change initiative?**
   A. Generate short-term wins
   B. Gather a guiding coalition
   C. Create a sense of urgency
   D. Develop a compelling vision

5. **Which of the following statements does *not* describe an effective change-implementation plan?**
   A. The plan is simple.
   B. The plan is created by the most qualified, top-level leaders.
   C. The plan is structured in achievable "chunks."
   D. The plan builds in flexibility.

6. **You want to begin identifying change resisters in your firm. Which of the following steps would you take first?**
   A. Ask managers to name employees they believe have the hardest time with change.
   B. Have your department conduct an employee opinion survey about change.
   C. Watch for absenteeism and other symptoms of stress.
   D. Determine where and how change will create pain in your organization.

7. **Human beings tend to go through a specific set of stages in reacting to change. Which of the following is *not* one of those stages?**
   A. Shock
   B. Offensive attack
   C. Acknowledgment
   D. Acceptance and adaptation

8. **People are best able to adapt to new realities when . . . ?**
   A. Nonwork aspects of their lives remain stable
   B. They are responding to a specific kind of change for the first time
   C. A change is presented as large-scale and affects an entire organization
   D. They feel confident that top management has developed well-thought-out plans for change

9. **Your company has decided to initiate a reduction in force. Which of the following is the best guidance you can give managers who have to lay off employees?**
   A. Meet with affected employees one on one, so they won't feel overwhelmed.
   B. Allow affected employees as much time as they need to say goodbye to colleagues.
   C. Let affected employees vent their emotions if they need to.
   D. Conduct termination interviews on Friday, so affected employees can have the weekend to recover.

10. **You're preparing to lead or facilitate change in your organization. Which three-step process would you use?**
    A. Prepare for change, align HR behind the business, and develop plans for transforming the corporate culture.
    B. Align HR behind the business, establish an empowerment program, and develop the change leadership team.
    C. Prepare for change, conduct a strategic HR analysis, and strengthen your understanding of the business.
    D. Conduct a strategic HR analysis, align HR behind the business, and prepare for change.

Answer Key

1. D: All of the above
   Chapter 2: Dimensions of Change

2. A: Leaders who have others' respect and who have earned a reputation for effectiveness
   Chapter 3: Is Your Organization Change-Ready?

3. B: A calmness in the face of unnerving new experiences
   Chapter 4: Are You and Your Employees Change-Ready?

4. C: Create a sense of urgency
   Chapter 5: Eight Steps to Change: A Systematic Approach

5. B: The plan is created by the most qualified, top-level leaders
   Chapter 6: Implementation

6. D: Determine where and how change will create pain in your organization
   Chapter 7: How Employees Respond to Change

7. B: Offensive attack
   Chapter 8: Helping Employees Adapt to Change

8. A: Nonwork aspects of their lives remain stable
   Chapter 9: Toward Continuous Change

9. C: Let affected employees vent their emotions if they need to
   Chapter 10: Common HR Change-Management Challenges for HR Professionals

10. D: Conduct a strategic HR analysis, align HR behind the business, and prepare for change
    Chapter 11: HR as Change Agent

- Leveraging synergies from internal teamwork and external partnerships and alliances

- Constantly renewing company offerings through innovative thinking

- Remaking organizational systems, structures, and cultures to encourage better flow of information and a willingness to take risks

The chapter also explained the components of a strategic approach to change management:

- Culture management

- Change acceleration

- Strategic decision making

- Market understanding

- Business and strategic planning

Finally, you learned about the dual role of HR professionals as change agents and facilitators, which some experts describe in terms of four functions: "scouts" (scanning the environment to identify the company's strengths, weaknesses, opportunities, and threats), "chess masters" (deploying human resources to best influence the outcome of a change initiatives), "cartographers" (providing a road map to help people navigate major change), and "architects" (rethinking the design of systems and processes for managing human performance).

Leveraging Chapter Insights: Critical Questions

- What forces of change are exerting the most impact on your company right now? What changes will your firm need to make to adapt to and benefit from these forces?

- Which of the new capabilities described in this chapter is your company best at? Which of these capabilities is it weakest in? How might you help your firm strengthen its weakest capabilities?

- In what ways do you currently support culture management, change acceleration, strategic decision making, market understanding, and business and strategic planning in your company? How might you provide even better support for these activities?

- Are you a talented change "scout," "chess master," "cartographer," and "architect"? If not, how can you improve your ability to play all four roles in your firm?

CHAPTER TWO

Dimensions of Change

Examining Types and Approaches

Key Topics Covered in This Chapter

- *An overview of the primary types of change programs*

- *A look at three ways to time change*

- *A discussion of two different approaches to change—one aims to increase shareholder value; the other, to improve a company's culture and employees' skills*

- *An evaluation of which approach to change is most appropriate*

B EFORE WE JUMP into the nitty-gritty details of managing change, it's useful to take a broad look at the kinds of change programs many companies initiate and the many different ways in which organizations approach the change-management process. By taking this broader view now, you'll find it easier to grasp and implement the specific guidelines you'll discover in the chapters that follow.

Types of Change Programs

Organizations typically respond to the challenges of new technologies, new competitors, new markets, and demands for greater performance with various change programs, each designed to overcome obstacles and enhance business performance. Generally, such programs fall into one of the following categories:

- **Structural change.** These programs treat the organization as a set of functional parts—a "machine." During structural change, top managers (often aided by consultants) attempt to reconfigure these parts to achieve greater overall performance. Mergers, acquisitions, consolidations, and divestiture of operating units are all examples of attempts at structural change.

- **Cost cutting.** Programs such as these focus on the elimination of nonessential activities and other methods for squeezing costs out of operations. Activities and operations that get little scrutiny during profitable years draw the attention of cost cutters when times grow tough.

- **Process change.** These programs focus on altering *how* things get done. Examples include reengineering a benefits-administration process, the company's approach to handling workers' compensation claims, or the way in which hiring decisions are made. Process change typically aims to make processes faster, more effective, more reliable, and/or less costly.

- **Cultural change.** These programs focus on the "human" side of the organization, such as a company's general approach to doing business or the relationship between managers and employees. A shift from command-and-control management to participative management is an example of cultural change.

- **Leadership change.** Such programs aim to reconfigure the organization's leadership—for example, by promoting former individual contributors into managerial positions, replacing current executives and managers with new ones from outside the company, and creating succession programs that establish a pipeline of qualified leaders who can step in when high-level leaders depart for retirement or other reasons.

None of these change programs is easy, nor is success ever assured. A structural change—such as the acquisition of a complementary business—might appear easy, since the entire deal can be handled by a small platoon of senior managers and consultants, with input from the board of directors. But such an operation results in a need for more amorphous changes, such as eliminating redundancies and getting the acquired units to work together smoothly. All of this can prove enormously difficult and time-consuming. And the record shows that few of these initiatives come close to meeting their supporters' expectations. On the other hand, a change that focuses on a discrete operation, such as improving the payroll-administration function, may be both easier to handle and more likely to succeed, since it involves relatively few activities. The employees involved in that function may be able to handle the job themselves, perhaps with a bit of coaching from a knowledge-able consultant or mentor within the company.

If your organization is contemplating a change program, think about which of the categories described above the initiative falls into. Ask yourself how the initiative is likely to affect the company overall. Envisioning potential stumbling blocks in advance could prevent difficult issues from arising during the change process and help ensure a successful operation.

Three Tactics for Timing Change

When companies launch change programs, they implement not only different *kinds* of change, but base them on different types of *timing*. Experts have identified three types of timing:[1]

- **Anticipatory change.** The organization looks ahead to possi-ble shifts in the business landscape. It attempts to figure out in advance what changes it will need to make to remain compet-itive once the contours of the landscape have been altered.

- **Reactive change.** The organization notices signs of change surfacing from customers, competitors, shareholders, employ-ees, and other critical stakeholders suggesting that it needs to change today.

- **Crisis change.** The signals of needed change have multiplied and intensified to the point at which the organization can't deny them. Competitors have already initiated major changes, and the consequences of "sitting on the sidelines" are now showing up in the firm's financial performance.

Each of these timing choices has advantages and disadvantages. For example, firms that make anticipatory changes tend to have stronger strategic capability—that is, they consistently distinguish themselves from competitors and stay ahead of the pack. That's because these companies have time to carefully work out strategies for change. On the other hand, without a crisis looming over the company, managers may feel less of a sense of urgency about implementing the required changes. Leaders who are advocating change may have difficulty being seen as credible.

Organizations that tend to initiate reactive change might be able to generate more of a sense of urgency among managers—because the corresponding environmental shifts are more imminent. However, owing to the faster pace with which they need to implement change, managers may have less time available to develop clear, focused strategies and careful analyses of the competition.

Finally, companies that wait until things reach a crisis before making necessary changes often generate the highest possible sense of urgency among managers. Yet they have almost no time to lay the groundwork for thoughtful, measured change. In addition, by the time crisis strikes, most companies' resources have been depleted. Costs—in the form of major layoffs, idled manufacturing plants, and a damaged reputation in the eyes of customers, suppliers, and society—can prove debilitating. And panicked leaders, under enormous time pressure, are focusing more on what worked in the past than on what new strategies may be best for the future.

Note that not all crisis change results from inaction. Sometimes, HR professionals may move to help a company evaluate the potential need for change, rather than waiting for the crisis point. At other times, the need for crisis change may arise because signals for change were not properly read. Or perhaps an unexpected event (for example, a natural disaster) has left a company no choice but to implement crisis change. Regardless of the impetus for this type of change, HR professionals need to anticipate how they and their company will respond in any crisis situation.

Companies can't anticipate every future alteration in the business landscape. But they can carefully consider the various tradeoffs associated with deciding whether to use anticipatory, reactive, or crisis change to remain competitive in their industry. The smarter a firm uses anticipatory change, the less likely it will have to resort to reactive or crisis change.

Two Different Approaches to Change

While there are many types of change programs, two very different goals typically drive a change initiative: *near-term economic improvement* or an *improvement in organizational capabilities*. Harvard Business School professors Michael Beer and Nitin Nohria coined the terms "Theory E" and "Theory O" to describe these two basic goals.[2]

Theory E: An Economic Approach

The explicit goal of Theory E change is to dramatically and rapidly increase shareholder value as measured by improved cash flow and share price. Popular notions of employee participation and the "learning organization" take a back seat to this overarching goal. Financial crisis usually triggers this approach to change. Driven to increase shareholder value, Theory E proponents rely heavily on mechanisms likely to increase short-term cash flow and share price. These mechanisms include performance bonuses, headcount reductions, asset sales, and strategic reordering of business units. Jack Welch's 25 percent headcount reduction at GE, and his subsequent "be number 1 or number 2 in your market or be sold" strategy are prime examples of actions stemming from a Theory E change process.

According to Theory E, all implicit contracts between the company and its employees, such as lifetime employment, are suspended during the change effort. Individuals and units whose activities fail to demonstrate tangible value creation—for example, corporate planning or R&D—become particularly vulnerable during such change initiatives.

The CEO and the executive team drive Theory E change from the top. Corporate departments, operating units, and employees involved in this approach are like pieces on management's strategic chessboard; they are rearranged or combined, and occasionally cashed out. Outside consultants provide advice to members of the inner circle. For example, strategy consultants help management identify and weigh its options, and valuation specialists and investment bankers arrange for asset sales and/or acquisitions. During such times, the HR department may obtain assistance from external specialists to handle major layoffs.

Theory O: An Organizational Capabilities Approach

We've all been told that the most successful and enduring organizations are those with dynamic, learning-oriented cultures and highly capable employees. Companies such as Intel, Microsoft, 3M, Schwab, and Merck come to mind. The goal of Theory O change is to develop an organizational culture that supports learning and a high-performance employee base.

Companies that follow this approach attempt to invigorate their cultures and capabilities by strengthening individual and organizational learning. This effort requires high levels of employee participation, flatter reporting structures, and strong bonds between the organization and its people. Because employee commitment to change and improvement are vital for Theory O change to work, implicit contracts with employees are considered too important to break—quite the opposite from what happens in the Theory E organization. For example, when Hewlett-Packard found itself stagnating in the early 1980s, it didn't jettison people to cut costs. Instead, it reduced bureaucracy and gave people and operating units greater autonomy. That approach was consistent with HP's time-honored tradition of valuing its people assets above all others.

An organization that banks on its culture and people to drive financial success is potentially incompatible with concentrated power and direction from the top. But leaders of Theory O change are less interested in driving the success themselves. Rather, they tend to encourage participation within the ranks and foster employee behaviors and attitudes that will sustain such change.

Which Is Most Appropriate—Theory E or Theory O?

If your organization is considering a major change program, you are probably wondering whether Theory E– or Theory O–type change is best. Unfortunately, the record shows that neither approach guarantees success. Theory E, aiming for rapid improvements in profitability, often succeeds in the short run, but it does so at the expense of future vitality. By decimating employee ranks, it leaves survivors demoralized and disloyal. Any commitment they had to the company and its goals evaporates. Ironically, the people the organization hopes to retain—the brightest and most marketable employees—are among the first to snap up severance packages and look for greener pastures.

Nor do Theory E's draconian measures always produce the desired results. A survey conducted after the last wave of corporate downsizings (from the late 1980s through the early 1990s) found that only 45 percent of downsizers reported higher operating profits.[3] Additional statistics further drive home the point that downsizing doesn't pay in the long run. One study revealed that during 1982–2000, companies that downsized achieved significantly lower cumulative returns on common stock in the two years following a downsizing initiative than companies that "upsized."[4]

Theory O is not an ideal solution either. Reorienting corporate culture around employee commitment and learning is a noble endeavor, but it is a multiyear proposition. A successful program may produce a smarter, more adaptive employee base in four to five years, but companies that need to effect major change fast cannot wait that long for results. Managers and employees, not to mention analysts and shareholders, simply aren't that patient.

Most companies studied by Beer and Nohria eschewed both pure Theory E and Theory O as solutions, preferring a mix of the two to suit their needs. Indeed, this may be the best path for your organization to follow (see "A Tale of Two Theories" for examples of the pitfalls of attempting to apply only one of the approaches). "Companies that effectively combine hard and soft approaches to change can reap big payoffs in profitability and productivity," the authors write. "Those companies are more likely to achieve a sustainable competitive advantage [and] . . . reduce the anxiety that grips whole societies in the face of corporate restructuring."[5]

A Tale of Two Theories

To illustrate Theory E and Theory O, Michael Beer and Nitin Nohria have described two companies in similar businesses that adopted almost pure forms of each archetype: Scott Paper used Theory E to enhance shareholder value, while Champion International used Theory O to achieve a cultural transformation aimed at increasing productivity and employee commitment. Here's how they described these initiatives to readers of the *Harvard Business Review*:

When Al Dunlap assumed leadership of Scott Paper in May 1994, he immediately fired 11,000 employees and sold off several businesses. . . . As he said in one of his speeches: "Shareholders are the number one constituency. Show me an annual report that lists six or seven constituencies, and I'll show you a mismanaged company." From a shareholder's perspective, the results of Dunlap's actions were stunning. In just 20 months, he managed to triple shareholder returns as Scott's market value rose from about $3 billion in 1994 to about $9 billion in 1995. . . . Champion's reform effort couldn't have been more different. CEO Andrew Sigler acknowledged that enhanced economic value was an appropriate target for management, but he believed that goal would be best achieved by transforming the behaviors of management, unions, and workers alike.

In the end, neither company achieved its goal. Dunlap was forced to sell a demoralized and ineffective organization to Kimberly-Clark, and a languishing Champion International was sold to UPM-Kymmene. These failures contrast sharply with the successes enjoyed by companies that skillfully integrated the two approaches.

Source: Michael Beer and Nitin Nohria, "Cracking the Code of Change," *Harvard Business Review* (May–June 2000): 135.

Beer and Nohria offer General Electric as an example where former CEO Jack Welch employed both approaches in turn. First he squeezed out all of the redundancies and under-performing units through draconian Theory E methods. He then followed with change initiatives designed to improve the competitiveness of the company's culture by making it faster, less bureaucratic, and more customer-focused—a Theory O move. As described by Dave Ulrich:

> By the late 1980s, GE was strategically strong, with thirteen major businesses, each lean, globally positioned, and number one or two in market share. Since the latter part of the 1980s, GE's management has focused on more fundamental culture change. Under the rubric [Work-Out], a number of initiatives involved GE employees in dismantling bureaucracies, making faster decisions, moving more quickly to serve customers, and getting rid of unnecessary work. Through town hall meetings in which employees worked with managers to identify and eliminate unnecessary work, GE worked to incorporate the values of speed, simplicity, and self-confidence into the organization's culture.[6]

In a sense, GE's method was to fix the "hardware" first through divestitures and consolidations. Once that job was completed, it turned its focus to the "software"—its employees and how they conducted their work.

Which approach is best for your particular situation? Only you and the other people who are familiar with the inner workings of your company can say with any authority. To help you think through the pros and cons of each theory, table 2-1 summarizes the two archetypal change approaches—and their combination—along six dimensions. You can tell a lot about the mind-set of your company's executive team, including yourself, by checking off how the team manages each of the six dimensions.

How to figure out which change philosophy predominates in your organization? Try your hand at filling out assessment tool 2-1 to see what insights you gain.

TABLE 2-1

Key Factors in Theory E and Theory O Change

Dimensions of Change	Theory E	Theory O	Theories E and O Combined
Goals	Maximize shareholder value	Develop organizational capabilities	Embrace the paradox between economic value and organizational capability
Leadership	Manage change from the top	Encourage participation from the bottom up	Set direction from the top and engage the people below
Focus	Emphasize structure and systems	Build up corporate culture: employees' behavior and attitudes	Focus simultaneously on the hard (structures and systems) and the soft (corporate culture)
Process	Plan and establish programs	Experiment and evolve	Plan for spontaneity
Reward system	Motivate through financial incentives	Motivate through commitment— use pay as fair exchange	Use incentives to reinforce change but not to drive it
Use of consultants	Consultants analyze problems and shape solutions	Consultants support management in shaping their own solutions	Consultants are expert resources who empower employees

Source: Michael Beer and Nitin Nohria, "Cracking the Code of Change," *Harvard Business Review* (May–June 2000): 137.

Summing Up

This chapter highlighted the different types of change initiatives observed in organizations:

- Structural change

- Cost cutting change

- Process change

- Cultural change

Assessment Tool 2-1
Assess Your Company's Change Philosophy

Does your company generally take the Theory E approach to change? The Theory O approach? Both? Consider the following questions in light of the six dimensions described in table 2-1.

1. **Goals:** In statements made during company meetings, in company publications, and in press releases and other external publications, do your company's other top managers seem to emphasize the importance of shareholder value or learning and a high-performing workforce? Or both? What are some examples of evidence suggesting a Theory E or Theory O approach to change—or a blend of both?

2. **Leadership:** Think about the various change programs that have been launched at your company. Are most of them managed from the top or driven by participants at lower levels of the company? Or do the most senior-level executives set the general direction for the programs while engaging people from below to drive the effort? What do you see, hear, and do that indicates how your company leads change?

The chapter also examined three ways of timing change:

- Crisis change

- Reactive change

- Anticipatory change

It also explored two different approaches that companies can take to pursue these changes:

3. **Focus:** When your company launches change initiatives, does it tend to add, remove, or try to improve reporting structures, systems, and processes? Does it focus on altering employees' attitudes and behaviors? Does it attempt to change things on both a structural *and* cultural level? How can you tell?

4. **Process:** In initiating change, does your company tend to create a plan and then stick to it or "play" with a number of different ideas at once? Or does it put plans in place that encourage people to experiment with various ideas for change? How do you know?

5. **Rewards:** What do people in your organization get rewarded for? The company's financial results? Positive changes in processes, culture, and other nonfinancial performance indicators? Commitment to the company's mission? What causes you to draw your conclusions about how your firm uses rewards?

6. **Consultants:** Does your company tend to outsource development and management of change programs to external consultants? Does it design its own change programs and then hire consultants to support implementation of the programs? What are some examples of actual events that inform your answers to these questions?

- Theory E change aims for a dramatic and rapid increase in shareholder value. It is driven from the top of the organization and makes heavy use of outside consultants. Theory E relies heavily on cost cutting, downsizing, and asset sales to meet its objectives.

- Theory O change aims to create higher performance by fostering a powerful culture and capable employees. It is characterized by high levels of employee participation and flatter organizational structure, and attempts to build bonds between the enterprise and its employees. Unlike Theory E, this approach to change is a long-term proposition.

The most successful companies seem to blend aspects of Theory E and Theory O change.

Leveraging Chapter Insights: Critical Questions

- What kinds of change programs does your company generally initiate? Structural? Cost cutting? Process? Cultural? In your view, should the organization alter its mix of change programs in any way? If so, why?

- Does your organization typically demonstrate anticipatory change? Reactive change? Crisis change? What advantages and disadvantages has the company experienced while timing change in these ways? Do you have ideas for how the organization might counter the disadvantages of anticipatory change—such as creating a higher sense of urgency, clarifying potential future issues facing the company, and building change advocates' credibility?

- Does your firm take a Theory E or Theory O approach to change—or does it blend these two approaches? Do you think a different approach to change would enable the company to enhance its performance? If so, what alterations would you advocate?

CHAPTER THREE

Is Your Organization Change-Ready?

Preparing for Companywide Change

Key Topics Covered in This Chapter

- *Why leaders must be respected and effective for change to happen*

- *The role of reward systems in organizational change-readiness*

- *The importance of a nonhierarchical culture in implementing change*

- *Tips on how an organization can become "change-ready"*

T H E information and advice given in this book will be of little use if your organization is not "change-ready." By change-ready, we mean that the firm's people and structures are prepared for and capable of change. An organization is change-ready when three major conditions are present:

1. Leaders are respected and effective.

2. The organization uses appropriate reward systems.

3. The organization is nonhierarchical and people are accustomed to collaborative work.

This chapter delves into these conditions in greater detail and explains how HR professionals can cultivate them in their companies.

Respected and Effective Leaders

Everything we know about management tells us that mediocre or downright bad bosses—people who are neither respected nor effective—are absolute deterrents to organizational performance. They cannot retain good employees, and they cannot motivate those who remain. A company can have terrific pay and benefits, employee-friendly policies, and all the other things that contribute to employee loyalty and retention, but a few bad-apple managers can spoil the barrel. In addition, inept leaders in key positions can thwart well-designed plans to improve performance. In writing about the problem of "C performers," or managers with less-than-stellar skills, Beth Axelrod, Helen Handfield-Jones, and Ed Michaels of McKinsey & Company pinpoint some of the key issues raised by mediocre or bad managers:

> [K]eeping C performers in leadership positions lowers the bar for everyone—a clear danger for any company that wants to create a performance-focused culture. C performers hire other C performers, and their continued presence discourages the people around them, makes the company a less attractive place for highly talented people, and calls into question the judgment of senior leaders.[1]

If your organization has lots of mediocre managers, don't expect to see any change program get very far. C performers are ineffective at motivating people to embark on difficult tasks. Help your firm's other executives cull out any C-performer managers in your company and replace them with effective and respected people. Considering doing the same with C performers in your own department. You'll move your organization a step closer to being change-ready.

Smart hiring can be a key to improving your company's leadership "bench strength." Claudio Fernández-Aráoz offers the suggestions shown below for identifying and attracting top-notch managers to your firm. Namely, Fernández-Aráoz advises executives to avoid ten "deadly traps" that can foil even the best-thought-out hiring efforts—and end up with a new manager being let go for mediocre performance.[2] You can apply these guidelines when you hire managers in your own department, as well as encourage other executives throughout your firm to use them while recruiting new managers to the company:

1. **Reacting:** hiring someone who's the polar opposite of a problem manager who was recently let go

2. **Having unrealistic expectations:** demanding too many contradictory qualities, such as "high-energy doer *and* thoughtful analyst"

3. **Evaluating people in absolute terms:** for example, describing "Joe" as a "good manager" without clarifying that he manages *processes* well, but not people

4. **Accepting people at face value:** not getting the full story of a candidate's background

5. **Believing references:** trusting references' input without determining their credibility

6. **Falling victim to the "just like me" bias:** giving the highest ratings to candidates who are just like you

7. **Making delegation gaffes:** assigning critical steps in the search process to ill-prepared staff

8. **Conducting unstructured interviews:** failing to prepare interview questions that reveal candidates' competencies

9. **Ignoring emotional intelligence:** failing to assess candidates' self-awareness, motivation, empathy, and social skills

10. **Caving in to political pressures:** hatching inappropriate agendas, such as hiring an executive's friend

How to avoid these traps? Fernández-Aráoz recommends these strategies:

- **Define the problem you need to solve through hiring.** Clarify the position's *current and future requirements,* driven by your firm's strategy. Translate these requirements into needed skills (e.g., comfort with uncertainty). Also list *required competencies* in behavioral terms and get consensus on the list. For example, "strategic vision" means the ability to inspire and guide others.

- **Creatively generate a candidate list.** Contact people who can recommend *several* quality candidates (e.g., a major supplier's CEO could recommend sales leaders). And consider unconventional candidate sources. (One president hired a director whom his own predecessor had fired!)

- **Methodically evaluate the candidates.** Conduct *structured interviews* in which you assess candidates' competencies through behavior-based questions. For instance, to measure team skills, ask, "Tell me about a time you led a particularly challenging team project." Also meet with references in *person* if possible. Describe the open job and ask pointed questions— such as "How has this candidate performed while facing similar challenges?"

Appropriate Reward Systems

In addition to having effective and respective leaders, change-ready organizations establish appropriate reward systems that encourage openness to change. Almost all fundamental changes in organizations involve some alterations in the way people are rewarded for performance.

Much academic research has reached what seems to be an obvious conclusion: a well-aligned compensation system rewards the adoption of the behaviors (or outcomes) you want throughout the organization and discounts the behaviors (or outcomes) you hope to discourage. If you want a clear example, you needn't look any farther than Nucor's steelmaking operations, where output and pay are closely linked, and where employees are more productive than steelworkers anywhere else.

Less obvious to change planners and leaders is *which* behaviors and outputs to reward. These decisions depend on the organization's situation. However, change leaders must think them through carefully. Making a mistake in the rewards regime can throw a monkey wrench into the works. So, to see if there are opportunities to make your organization more change-ready, check the alignment between the firm's rewards system and the behaviors that company leaders want to encourage. Business professor Edward Lawler makes the point that different reward systems are more appropriate at different phases of a change initiative.[3] For example:

- Performance-based pay plans, such as stock options and profit sharing, are most appropriate for motivating organizational readiness for change.

- As change is being implemented, bonuses for achieving performance targets and successful implementation can prove especially useful.

- Finally, once change has been effected, the organization may want to shift to a pay-for-performance regime that focuses on the strategic performance and the attraction/retention of talented people.

But rewards alone cannot produce desired changes if the people charged with effecting change lack the knowledge, information, and power they need to do the job. Thus, rewards must be part of a larger package of transformational levers including effective leadership, smart hiring, training, communication, and so forth. Moreover, rewards can take many different forms in addition to financial incentives for desired behaviors and performance. In fact, some experts argue that raises, promotions, bonuses, and other "extrinsic" rewards only encourage people to wait for the *next* payoff. These experts maintain that "intrinsic" rewards provide a much more powerful motivation for demonstrating the enduring behaviors and attitudes required for the company to compete—such as the learning, creativity, and collaboration needed to help a much-needed change initiative succeed.

For example, some experts advocate enriching people's jobs—providing challenging work based on what excites and stretches employees. People are *most* motivated by work that stimulates them while also furthering company goals, so suggests ways in which managers can help their employees channel their passions in the service of business objectives. This alignment requires managers to determine what drives individual employees most powerfully (a desire for interpersonal interaction? recognition?). Managers must then invite workers to suggest ways in which they can obtain these rewards through job responsibilities that support the corporate strategy.

A Nonhierarchical Organization

If an organization needs to undergo economically driven change by selling off assets, downsizing the workforce, and reorganizing around a more manageable core, a hierarchical structure may not be an impediment. In fact, a highly managed, command-and-control structure may be optimal for such an initiative to take hold. But other types of change—of processes and culture—require something much different.

For such changes to succeed, an organization must streamline or eliminate rigid hierarchies. Yet this process itself is akin to swimming upstream. Here's why:

- In hierarchical organizations, decisions are made at the top and passed down through intermediaries. But many people resist solutions imposed by individuals whom they perceive as lacking familiarity with day-to-day operations.

- Organizations that aim to change need a certain number of entrepreneurial employees—people who like to try new things and who are comfortable with taking risks. But hierarchical firms have few such entrepreneurial spirits.

- Hierarchy protects two enemies of change: bureaucracy (the protectors of "how we do things around here") and a sense of entitlement among employees—that is, a sense that "If I just stay in my little cubicle and continue doing what I've always done, my job will be guaranteed."

- Effective change demands collaboration between willing and motivated parties. Unfortunately, hierarchical companies are better at telling people what to do than at getting employees to collaborate.

The problem with hierarchy is that it simply doesn't facilitate collaborative work—one of the important skills that employees must have in a change-ready organization. When hierarchy dominates the culture, corporate commissars do all the thinking, control access to information, and tell everyone what to do. Under these circumstances, collaboration feels like an unnatural act.

There are two ways to overcome the problem of hierarchy. First, HR and other leaders can push the organization toward a more decentralized business model in which individual units have greater autonomy. This in itself would be a major "Theory O" change initiative. If that organizational makeover is not possible in the short run, then leaders might follow the second course: creating opportunities for collaboration between people in different units and at different levels. For example, managers might set up cross-functional teams to deal with key issues such as employee benefits or new performance-management approaches.

Wondering how hierarchical your organization might be? To find out, try your hand at assessment tool 3-1.

Shaping a Change-Ready Organization

If your organization isn't change-ready, you can take steps to model change-readiness in your own department. Equally important, you can help other managers and executives throughout your company both demonstrate change-readiness themselves and encourage it in their direct reports. The following guidelines can help:

Help Managers Assess Their Units' Change-Readiness

Although an organization as a whole may be unprepared for change, specific units may be ready to go—that is, they have respected and effective leaders, and people in those units are accustomed to working together in collaborative ways. Ask managers throughout your organization whether they believe their units

Assessment Tool 3-1
How Hierarchical Is Your Company?

For each statement below, circle the number that best expresses your opinion of how accurately the statement describes your company. "1" indicates "not at all true"; "5" indicates "very true."

1. In my organization, decisions are made at the top and handed down through intermediaries.

   1   2   3   4   5

2. Some people have expressed a concern that company leaders lack familiarity with day-to-day operations.

   1   2   3   4   5

3. My organization has few managers and employees who exhibit an entrepreneurial spirit.

   1   2   3   4   5

4. Employees believe that if they continue doing their work in the same ways as before, they deserve to keep working for the firm.

   1   2   3   4   5

5. Higher-ups control access to information in the company.

   1   2   3   4   5

6. Numerous people strive to protect the status quo—or the ways in which work has always been done in the company.

   1   2   3   4   5

7. Many employees wait to be told what to do rather than taking initiative themselves.

   1   2   3   4   5

Continued

8. Most employees don't engage comfortably and effectively in collaborative work.

   1   2   3   4   5

9. We seem to have the most difficulty implementing change initiatives that involve improving work processes or enhancing our corporate culture.

   1   2   3   4   5

10. The company emphasizes symbols of status and power, such as opulent offices for higher-level managers.

    1   2   3   4   5

Calculating Your Score:
To calculate your score, add up the numbers you circled.

Interpreting Your Score:
The higher your score, the more hierarchical your organization may be.

Score 38–50: Your organization is strongly hierarchical, which may be constraining its change-readiness. Finding ways to overcome the hierarchical culture would go a long way toward improving the company's change-readiness.

Score 24–37: Your organization has some of the characteristics that define a hierarchical company. You might consider whether these characteristics are hampering collaborative work throughout the firm—an ability that's essential to change-readiness.

Score 10–23: Your organization seems to demonstrate few of the characteristics associated with a hierarchical culture. Employees likely feel comfortable engaging in collaborative work, which is crucial for change-readiness.

have these characteristics. If you're leading a change program, use these units as test beds for your initiative.

Encourage Managers to Demonstrate Participative Approaches to Everyday Business

Model and encourage the "habits" of participative work. Specifically, ask managers and executives whether they exhibit the following behaviors:

- They push decision making down to the lowest possible levels in their department.

- They share information freely.

- They make communication a two-way street—by talking, but also listening.

- They avoid or discourage unnecessary symbols of hierarchy and unequal status—such as high- and low-status offices.

- They encourage participatory decision making from employees.

- They get into the trenches with frontline employees.

- They give people practice in collaborative work between functions by attacking projects and problems through cross-functional teams.

- They help people see the "why" of change, and work with them to discover the "what."

In addition to asking other managers and executives how much they exhibit these behaviors, evaluate your own performance on these criteria. Demonstrating the same behaviors you're encouraging in others further strengthens your credibility and enables you to earn your peers' trust.

Assess *Complacency in Your Organization*

Complacency—an overall sense in a company that everything's just fine and that there's no need to challenge the status quo—can kill a change initiative. Thus identifying and battling companywide complacency count among the most crucial strategies for making your organization change-ready. To get a sense of your organization's overall readiness for change, consider the degree of complacency characterizing the company. Table 3-1, which draws from John Kotter's thinking about organizational change-readiness, helps you identify key signs of this major obstacle to change-readiness.

TABLE 3-1

Is Your Organization Complacent?

Signs of Complacency	Examples
There is no highly visible crisis.	The company is not losing money; no big layoffs are threatened.
The company measures itself against low standards.	The company compares itself to the industry average, not to the industry leader.
Organizational structure focuses attention on narrow functional goals instead of broad business performance.	Marketing has one measurement criterion; manufacturing has another that is unrelated. Only the CEO uses broader measures (return on invested capital, economic value added, etc.).
Planning and control systems are rigged to make it easy for everyone to make their functional goals.	The typical manager or employee can work for months without encountering an unsatisfied or frustrated customer or supplier.
Performance feedback is strictly internal. Feedback from customers, suppliers, and shareholders is not encouraged.	The culture dictates that external feedback is either without value or likely to be uninformed. "Customers really don't know what they want. We do."
Evidence that change is needed results in finger-pointing.	"It's manufacturing's problem, not ours."
Management focuses on marginal issues.	"The ship is sinking. Let's rearrange the deck chairs."
The culture sends subliminal messages of success.	Plush furnishings, wood paneling, and fine art adorn corporate offices.
Management believes its own press releases and mythology.	"We are the greatest ad agency in the country. We set the standard for our industry."

Source: Adapted from John P. Kotter, *Leading Change* (Boston: Harvard Business School Press, 1996), 39–41.

If you've identified a significant degree of complacency in your organization, begin to address it by presenting your concerns to other executives and leaders. Once identified, complacency must then be fought on an individual level—something you'll learn more about in chapter 4.

Summing Up

Few change initiatives can succeed if the organization is not change-ready. This chapter described several characteristics of change-readiness that your company should possess before you launch a change initiative:

- **The organization has effective and respected leaders.** Leaders who lack those qualities cannot get people to change. If you can replace ineffective leaders, do so.

- **The organization has a nonhierarchical structure.** Hierarchy may present no impediment to a strictly economically driven change program, but it is a barrier to all others. Managers must either reduce the hierarchy or work around it by giving people collaborative work assignments.

In addition, the chapter offered several suggestions for making an organization change-ready:

- Assess individual units' change-readiness.

- Demonstrate and develop more participative approaches to everyday business.

- Assess organizationwide complacency.

Leveraging Chapter Insights: Critical Questions

- How would you describe your organization's change-readiness? In your view, is the company overall prepared for change— or not?

- Within the company, which units do you perceive as the *most* change ready? Why? Based on your assessment, which change initiatives would you consider trying out in these units?

- Look around your department—at the way work spaces are set up and the way people do their work every day. Which (if any) signs of hierarchy do you see? If your company is seeking to initiate a change for reasons other than economic urgency, what steps could you take to streamline or eliminate hierarchical structures?

- What steps could you take to strengthen leadership throughout the organization?

- How complacent does your company seem to be? On what observations have you based your assessment of the organization's complacency?

CHAPTER FOUR

Are You and Your Employees Change-Ready?

Preparing for Individual Change

Key Topics Covered in This Chapter

- *Characteristics of change-ready individuals*

- *The importance of motivation in individual change-readiness*

- *Steps HR executives and managers can take to challenge complacency, give people a voice, and drive out fear—to motivate employees to embrace change*

T H E right leadership, reward systems, and organizational culture all strongly determine whether a company is change ready. But *individual* change-readiness—the willingness and ability of every employee in the company to accept, embrace, and support change—provides the cornerstone for organizational change-readiness. If each person who works in your company isn't change-ready, even the best leaders, incentives, and cultural characteristics won't help your company respond to new business realities.

What do change-ready individuals look like? And how can HR professionals make themselves change-ready—and help others do the same? Let's consider these questions.

Characteristics of Change-Ready Individuals

Psychologists Robert Kriegel and David Brandt maintain that change-ready people don't have to be "superstars." But they do need to cultivate the following personal characteristics:[1]

- **Passion:** feeling excited and challenged by new possibilities; relishing new experiences; having intensity and determination

- **Resourcefulness:** making the most of any situation and using resources at hand to create plans

- **Optimism:** having a positive view of the future

- **Adventurousness:** wanting to take risks and to pursue the unknown

- **Adaptability:** being able to shift expectations in the face of new realities and rebound from adversity quickly

- **Confidence:** believing in one's own ability to handle a difficult situation

- **Tolerance for ambiguity:** being able to live with uncertainty and surprises

So, you've read the list of traits that characterize change-ready individuals. Do any—or all—of these traits describe you? If you're going to help the men and women in your organization become change-ready, you'll need to assess and possibly enhance your own change-readiness. Take the test in assessment tool 4-1 to get a sense of how change-ready you are.

The Importance of Motivation

When an individual possesses the characteristics of change-readiness, he or she has the most important change-ready trait of all: motivation to change aspects of his or her organization. For many people, motivation stems from tangible dissatisfaction with the status quo and an eagerness for something measurably better. Motivated people often experience a certain level of nervousness, fear, or discomfort—but also a clear sense of *urgency* for change.

The quality revolution led by the late W. Edwards Deming demonstrated, on a broad scale, how individuals' attitudes toward the status quo can either pave the way for change, or hold change at arm's length. Deming was a protégé of Walter Shewhart, who developed the theory and practice of statistical process control (SPC) in the 1930s at AT&T's Western Electric division. Deming diffused SPC principles to the wider world of U.S. manufacturing during the years of World War II. However, to his disappointment,

Assessment Tool 4-1
Are You Change-Ready?

For each statement below, circle the number that best describes how accurately that statement describes you or your beliefs. "1" indicates "Not at all true"; "6" indicates "Very true."

1. I prefer the familiar to the unknown.

    1   2   3   4   5

2. I rarely second-guess myself.

    1   2   3   4   5

3. I'm unlikely to change plans once they're set.

    1   2   3   4   5

4. I can't wait for the day to get started.

    1   2   3   4   5

5. I believe in not getting your hopes too high.

    1   2   3   4   5

6. If something's broken, I'll find a way to fix it.

    1   2   3   4   5

7. I get impatient when there are no clear answers.

    1   2   3   4   5

8. I'm inclined to establish routines and stay with them.

    1   2   3   4   5

9. I can make any situation work for me.

    1   2   3   4   5

10. When something important doesn't work out, it takes me time to adjust.

    1   2   3   4   5

11. I have a hard time relaxing and doing nothing.

    1   2   3   4   5

12. If something can go wrong, it usually does.

    1   2   3   4   5

13. When I get stuck, I'm inclined to improvise solutions.

    1   2   3   4   5

14. I get frustrated when I can't get a grip on something.

    1   2   3   4   5

15. I prefer work that is familiar and within my comfort zone.

    1   2   3   4   5

16. I can handle anything that comes along.

    1   2   3   4   5

17. Once I've made up my mind, I don't easily change it.

    1   2   3   4   5

18. I push myself to the max.

    1   2   3   4   5

19. My tendency is to focus on what can go wrong.

    1   2   3   4   5

20. When people need solutions to problems, they call on me.

    1   2   3   4   5

21. When an issue is unclear, my impulse is to clarify it right away.

    1   2   3   4   5

22. It pays to stay with the tried and true.

    1   2   3   4   5

Continued

23. I focus on my strengths and not my weaknesses.

    1   2   3   4   5

24. I find it hard to give up on something, even if it's not working out.

    1   2   3   4   5

25. I'm restless and full of energy.

    1   2   3   4   5

26. Things rarely work out the way you want them to.

    1   2   3   4   5

27. My strength is to find ways around obstacles.

    1   2   3   4   5

28. I can't stand to leave things unfinished.

    1   2   3   4   5

29. I prefer the main highway to the backroad.

    1   2   3   4   5

30. My faith in my abilities is unshakeable.

    1   2   3   4   5

31. When in Rome, do as the Romans do.

    1   2   3   4   5

32. I'm a vigorous and passionate person.

    1   2   3   4   5

33. I'm more likely to see problems than opportunities.

    1   2   3   4   5

corporate leaders abandoned and largely forgot those principles in the post-war era, when U.S. business found itself essentially unchallenged in the world. American manufacturing was satisfied, complacent, and comfortable—and had little interest in Deming's quality principles.

34. I look in unusual places to find solutions.

   1   2   3   4   5

35. I don't perform well when there are vague expectations and goals.

   1   2   3   4   5

Calculating Your Score:

This assessment measures the following key change-readiness traits. You're highly change-ready if your score on each trait falls between 22 and 26.

- **Resourcefulness:** Add up your scores on questions 6, 13, 20, 27, and 34.

- **Optimism:** Add up your scores on questions 5, 12, 19, 26, and 33. Subtract your total from 35.

- **Adventurousness:** Add up your scores on questions 1, 8, 15, 22, and 29. Subtract your total from 35.

- **Passion:** Add up your scores on questions 4, 11, 18, 25, and 32.

- **Adaptability:** Add up your scores on questions 3, 10, 17, 24, and 31. Subtract your total from 35.

- **Confidence:** Add up your scores on questions 2, 9, 16, 23, and 30.

- **Tolerance for ambiguity:** Add up your scores on questions 7, 14, 21, 28, and 35. Subtract your total from 35.

SOURCE: Robert Kriegel and David Brandt. *Sacred Cows Make the Best Burgers: Developing Change-Ready People and Organizations* (New York: Warner Books, 1996), 276–279.

Halfway around the world, however, America's competitors were extremely change-ready. Japan's industrial base had been flattened by the Allied bombings. The tiny island nation had few resources, and its products were viewed as shoddy and poorly designed. Worse, millions of its people were unemployed. Everyone in Japan knew that industrial revitalization was the only way out of this desperate situation. And Deming, a prophet ignored in his own land, offered a blueprint for success. As described by Richard Luecke in his book of history lessons for modern managers:

> Deming told the Japanese leaders that following [the SPC] approach would result in a "chain reaction" of good things for their companies. Improved quality would result in decreased cost (less rework, fewer delays, less scrappage), which would result in improved productivity, which would lead to the capture of markets, business survival, and more jobs.[2]

Eager and ready for change, Japan's industrial leaders embraced Deming's gospel on manufacturing quality and got workers and managers at all levels involved. Between 1950 and 1970, almost 15,000 engineers and many more thousands of factory supervisors were educated by Deming and others in the principles of statistical process control. Quality became something of an industrial religion in Japan, and Deming was its high priest.

The quality movement transformed Japanese industry, and those changes stuck. Before long, Japanese manufacturers managed to take over the motorcycle market, the small-car market, the market for inexpensive wristwatches, and the consumer electronics market. From those beachheads, they began moving upstream into computers, high-end timepieces, and luxury automobiles. They also won numerous awards for excellence in design and reliability. And consumers discovered that Japanese-made products, paradoxically, offered higher quality *and* lower cost.

Ironically, the United States—the nation that invented SPC—didn't begin to adopt quality methods with any real commitment until the late 1970s, when Ford Motor Company's Donald Peterson hired Deming to teach his people SPC principles. What made the men and women of Ford change-ready? It's simple. The company was in a death spiral; it was losing money hand over fist, and the Ford name had become an acronym for "Fix Or Repair Daily." Both management and rank-and-file employees knew in their bones that something had to change. Unlike Ford employees, the people who worked for cross-town rival General Motors remained complacent. For another five years, they continued to bask in the delusion that everything was just fine. In fact, when GM's own Quality & Reliability staff confronted top managers with the depth of the company's quality problems, the managers dismissed their study. The CEO and his circle remained firmly convinced that GM was the world's finest automaker, and the company against which all others had to be measured.[3] Only a harsh awakening would launch GM into the change it required.

Eventually, U.S. manufacturers widely embraced SPC principles—but only after employees at many levels had lost their complacency and were ready to receive them.

HR Professionals: Key Motivational Players

As an HR professional, you serve as a key player in motivating individuals throughout your organization to embrace change. For one thing, you exert a direct impact on the men and women of your own department or division by modeling change-readiness yourself. But even more important, you can—and often must—help peers throughout the company motivate *their* employees to embrace change. How? Through informal conversations, more formal workshops or discussions about the power of motivation, and coaching, you can arm executives and managers with the concepts, tools, and techniques needed to encourage change-readiness among their direct reports. However you convey these ideas and tactics, experts suggest focusing your efforts on the three themes: challenging complacency, empowering employees to have a voice in and to gain a sense of ownership of change initiatives, and driving out fear of change. The following sections shed additional light on these themes.

Challenge Complacency

Many successful change programs grow out of crisis. Ford's "change-or-die" story also unfolded at Continental Airlines, Harley-Davidson, the Martin guitar company, IBM, and many other firms. This situation raises an important question: Do people have to wait for a crisis before they become change-ready? According to Harvard Business School professor Mike Beer, the answer is no. He believes that all managers—whether they're facilitating change or initiating it—can raise concerns about a current problematic situation and challenge the complacency that fosters it—without resorting to "crisis mode" tactics. Consider sharing the following guidelines from Beer with executives and managers throughout your firm:[4]

1. **Use information about the organization's competitive situation to generate discussion with employees about current and prospective problems.** Top managers, Beer says, often fail to understand why employees aren't concerned about productivity, customer service, or costs. Too often, this lack of concern stems from managers' failure to put employees in touch with the relevant data. But without that data, everything *appears* fine.

2. **Create opportunities for employees to educate executives and managers about the problems they experience.** In some cases, top managers are out of touch with the business's weaknesses or emerging threats. But frontline employees understand these things through their daily experiences on the factory floor or in their face-to-face dealings with customers. If your company has this problem, devise and suggest ways in which top executives and managers can improve the ways in which they communicate with frontline people.

   For example, suggest to managers that they hold weekly "brown bag" sessions at which a selected employee makes a presentation to the group on production problems he or she has encountered on the manufacturing line, or on a specific type of difficulty experienced with serving a key customer. The group can then discuss possible causes of the problems and brainstorm potential solutions. These kinds of meetings help to keep managers informed, as well as communicate the message that challenging complacency is everyone's job.

3. **Create dialogue on the data.** Providing data to employees is one thing. Encouraging dialogue about the data is something

entirely different—and a lot more productive. In discussing data about your company's situation with employees, management needs to aim for a joint understanding of company problems. Suggest that they invite dialogue participants to share and test their assumptions and their diagnoses of the company's problems.

4. **Set high standards—then expect people to meet them.** Remind managers throughout your firm that when they set high standards for performance, behavior, and attitude, they help create dissatisfaction with the current standards. Complacency is a major barrier to change. When people feel comfortable with the way things are, they become oblivious to things that need changing. Encourage executives and managers to challenge complacency in themselves *and* their employees at every opportunity!

Give People a Voice

Having a voice empowers people to act—an essential ability in change-ready individuals. Richard Axelrod writes:

> *The cornerstone of any democratic process is voice—the power to be heard and to influence outcomes. Maximizing voice means widening the circle of involvement to encompass those likely to be affected by the change process, including those who might be opposed or who think differently. When people really believe their voice counts, a critical mass for change spontaneously emerges. But in companies that lack interactive discourse, it's harder to mobilize the energy and the innovation required to reverse sagging fortunes.[5]*

John Kotter makes the point that employees generally won't help—or cannot help—with a change effort if they feel relatively powerless or voiceless. He has also identified barriers to empowerment that the rest of us are likely to overlook. (See figure 4-1.) An organization's formal structure is one such barrier. For example, if a company's goal or vision is to "focus on the customer," an organizational structure that fragments resources and responsibilities

FIGURE 4-1

Barriers to Empowerment

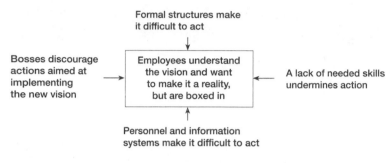

Formal structures make
it difficult to act

Bosses discourage
actions aimed at
implementing
the new vision

Employees understand
the vision and want
to make it a reality,
but are boxed in

A lack of needed skills
undermines action

Personnel and information
systems make it difficult to act

Source: John P. Kotter, *Leading Change* (Boston: Harvard Business School Press, 1996), 102.

Tips for Empowering People

Empowered employees are change-ready employees. To help peers throughout your firm to empower the people who work for them, offer the following guidelines. Apply these same strategies with your own employees. Each guideline below is followed by an illustration of how an HR executive or manager might apply the guideline.

- **Encourage and demonstrate innovative thinking.** You read an article about a radical new way to measure the financial impact of the company's intangible assets, and initiate a series of meetings with the executive team to discuss the potential pros and cons of the methodology.

- **Show respect for others' perspectives and ideas.** When a payroll administrator shares her idea about streamlining payroll services, you take time to listen to her thoughts and to explore the idea's ramifications.

- **Delegate; don't micromanage.** A benefits administrator complains to you about a disagreement he has had with his supervisor. Rather than taking on the problem yourself, you ask him how he plans to deal with the problem.

into disconnected silos will impede individuals' change-readiness. Likewise, a structure built on phalanxes of middle managers will probably block any effort to empower lower-level employees.

If you're serious about helping executives and managers in your organization enable employees to become change-ready, you'll have to assist in eliminating or lowering these barriers. Start with your own people. And look for opportunities to model similar behaviors for other executives and managers in your company. Whether you're leading a change effort or helping others do so, the "Tips for Empowering People" can provide you with additional guidelines.

- **Extend trust, and assume that others have the company's best interests at heart and genuinely want to help.** When the marketing manager complains about a new policy you've proposed, you resist the temptation to assume that she's just "being negative" or that she "has never respected what HR does." Instead, you invite her to share the thinking behind her concerns, and you point out ways in which you both want to see the company succeed.

- **Be flexible, and encourage flexibility in others.** After months of long, grueling strategy-formulation meetings, several other members of your company's executive team change their minds about how to define the company's competitive strategy. You remain open to the idea of redefining the strategy, and willingly explore the possible impact the changed definition will have on the HR group's strategy.

- **Demonstrate and encourage risk-taking, and look for lessons learned in any failures.** Your division group decides to install a new HR technology, and the effort ends in disaster. You take a deep breath and set up a series of meetings to explore what went wrong and identify what can be learned from the experience.

Drive Out Fear

The quality methodology Deming developed included fourteen points for effective management. One of those points urged managers to drive fear out of the workplace. A little bit of fear can help create the sense of urgency needed for individual change-readiness. But a *lot* of fear can paralyze people—rendering them incapable of change. Fear makes people want to avoid risks, hunker down, and keep their mouths shut about problems in the company. An atmosphere of fear hides the truth and keeps people from coming to grips with needed change.

Consider this example: Back in the early 1980s, before General Motors' leadership faced up to its quality problems, a group of managers and engineers conducted a study to determine what had gone wrong with the company's X-car and J-car projects, which had suffered numerous quality problems in their early production years. As Gregory Watson described in his book *Strategic Benchmarking*:

> *J-car veterans purged themselves in these [interview] sessions, describing how the pressure to keep to schedule and avoid reporting bad news to top management had led them to take shortcuts, compromise on quality, and even fudge test results on the J-car. It was revealed that when then-President and CEO James McDonald arrived with his entourage at the Arizona test track to try out the pre-production J-car, he unknowingly got behind the wheel of a vehicle whose engine had been secretly souped up and filled with special fuel to conceal its anemic performance. The test track itself had been redesigned during the previous few days to eliminate grades the car could not master.*[6]

Obviously, people can't be change-ready when they're gripped with fear. For example, men and women living in despotic nations know that the best way to survive is to shut up, follow orders, and cover up mistakes. But before long, these same countries find themselves outpaced by their more open and change-ready rivals. Companies are no different. Employees at all levels must feel free to challenge the status quo, identify problems, and suggest solutions— even when their views conflict with those of the firm's leadership.

They must also feel free to try new things without fear of retribu-
tion if they fail.

When people feel empowered, they feel less fearful—because
they have the sense that they can take action to control their fates.
So encourage managers to take steps to empower their own people—and do the same with your staff. You'll make major progress
in helping to reduce fear throughout your organization. John L.
Bennett offers these tips for driving out fear.[7] You can apply these
guidelines yourself, as well as remind other managers do the same
with their employees.

- **Accept change yourself.** It's virtually impossible to lead
  others through change if you don't have the ability to embrace
  the change yourself. Think about your own responses to a particular change. Ask yourself how readily you accepted it, what
  you resisted, and how you expressed that resistance. Use your
  insights from these questions to help your employees accept
  change—while realizing that everyone deals with change in
  his or her own way. In addition, encourage other executives or
  managers to assess their own responses to change and use the
  resulting insights to help their employees embrace change.

- **Invite people to help develop change-implementation plans.**
  By participating actively in this process, employees feel a
  stronger sense of ownership over and pride in the results. The
  more active involvement people have in change execution, the
  readier they'll be for the next change. For example, if you've
  decided to decentralize the HR function, be sure to ask for
  ideas on how to implement the plan from key people who
  will be most affected by this change.

- **Track and report progress on a change initiative.** When
  managers share news—good and not so good—of progress on
  a change effort, celebrate small victories, and address problems
  promptly, they enable employees to receive immediate and
  ongoing feedback on how they're doing. To illustrate, suppose
  your HR group has begun using a new technology—and the

HR In Action: Cultivating Change-Readiness at ConferNow

Virginia Packer, acting head of HR at ConferNow, a conference-management company, knew she needed to take decisive steps to cultivate change-readiness among the firm's employees. As a result of a recent economic downturn and the global war on terror, business travel had dried up—taking conference registrations with them. To survive, ConferNow had no choice but to trim staff, freeze pay raises and hiring, and redeploy individual workers within the company. Executives were even considering declaring bankruptcy.

Packer began her change-readiness effort by holding a companywide meeting at which she explained—in hard, cold numbers—the challenges confronting ConferNow. People's eyes widened as, for the first time, they saw what declining conference registrations meant in terms of the company's revenues and cash flow.

road to change has been rocky. Take time to identify what has gone *well* as well as where problems have cropped up, and express your appreciation for any gains.

- **Develop strategies for coping with resistance.** For example, perhaps some employees are resisting a new benefits policy because they find the new procedures for selecting a primary care physician and submitting medical claims confusing. In this case, you might encourage your benefits manager to lay out a clear set of instructions for putting the policy into practice.

- **Regularly remind people of the benefits of change.** By keeping the image of the good things that will come from change in the forefront of people's minds, managers help them become more change-ready. For instance, by frequently delin-

After a moment in which everyone studied the numbers in stunned silence, Packer warmly expressed her confidence in the company's ability to pull out of the slump. Then she challenged people to identify ways they could help. The responses proved rich and varied. For example, several people who had wanted to begin working part-time offered to cut back their hours as one way to trim expenses. Others expressed interest in investing in the company's stock. Still others laid out plans for contacting long-time customers to get ideas for potential new customers who might appreciate information about Pegasus' conferences.

Packer's change-readiness strategy paid off. Though the business environment remained tough, ConferNow's revenues perked up over the next three years, and the company survived. Perhaps even more crucially, Packer had infused the workforce with a desire to pitch in, contribute ideas, and commit to the firm's future. Such cohesion and change-readiness can be more valuable than any specific solution to a problem. It's a rare, intangible asset that the company can leverage during any time of change.

SOURCE: Telephone conversation with author, April 15, 2004

eating the benefits of adopting the proposed new medical claims procedures (such as quicker payment of claims or wider selection of physicians), your benefits manager can boost his chances of gaining acceptance of the procedures from employees.

- **Help people learn and grow.** All change requires people to learn new skills. That takes time, patience, direction, support, and coaching. The more you and other managers can provide these, the more change-readiness you can cultivate in others.

"HR In Action: Cultivating Change-Readiness at ConferNow" provides a striking illustration of how HR can act to motivate an organization for change.

Summing Up

In this chapter, you discovered the characteristics of change-ready individuals:

- Passion

- Resourcefulness

- Optimism

- Adventurousness

- Adaptability

- Confidence

- Tolerance for ambiguity

You also learned that motivation plays a vital part in individual change-readiness. Change-ready people are sufficiently dissatisfied with the status quo that they are willing to make the effort and accept the risks involved with doing something new. Even in the absence of a crisis, good managers can get people motivated to change.

In addition, the chapter offered several suggestions for how HR professionals can help individuals become change-ready:

- Challenge complacency.

- Give people a voice.

- Drive out fear.

Leveraging Chapter Insights: Critical Questions

- In what ways are *you* change-ready? In what ways are you change-resistant? What steps might you take to strengthen specific characteristics of change-readiness?

- How would you gauge the change-readiness of various individuals and groups in your company? What strategies might you suggest to peer managers to turn change-resistant individuals and groups into change-ready employees?

- Have you ever witnessed or worked for a manager who was able to cultivate change-readiness in employees? If so, how did he or she do it? What new behaviors and attitudes resulted?

CHAPTER FIVE

Eight Steps to Change

A Systematic Approach

Key Topics Covered in This Chapter

- *A description of an eight-step change process*

- *An explanation of the roles that HR professionals play during this process*

- *Tips on mistakes to avoid while implementing this process*

I F YOU'VE BEEN around corporations for any length of time, you've probably seen the launch of many change programs. Here's a typical scenario:

All employees are assembled in the cafeteria, where the CEO, flanked by managers from various functions, delivers a speech on yet another plan to make your company more productive and profitable. In years past, the company implemented plans for quality circles, service excellence, a pay-for-performance system, and process reengineering. Today it's The New Thing. The CEO then touts the virtues of the latest supposed panacea, points to a handful of companies that have used it to revitalize their performance, and describes what it can do here. Eventually pizza is served and everyone goes back to work, muttering "Here we go again."

If this little scenario sounds less than promising, let's speculate on some reasons why. The fact is, most people on the receiving end of change initiatives are probably thinking:

- "Why is this important?"

- "What's in it for me?"

- "How do these managers know what the company's problems are? They haven't even bothered to ask *us*."

- "Do they really think they can change this entire company at once?"

- "How much of our time and their money will they sink into this black hole?"

If this scenario seems overly contrived and pessimistic, consider this: In aggregate, the scorecard for change programs is very disappointing. By some estimates, 70 percent of change initiatives fail to meet their objectives.[1] As author John Kotter once put it, "If you were to grade them using the old fashioned A, B, C, D, and F, I'd be surprised if an impartial jury would give 10 percent of these efforts an A. But I'm not saying that 90 percent deserve a D either. What is tragic is that there are so many C-pluses. It's one thing to get a C-plus on a paper; it's another when millions of dollars or thousands of jobs are at stake."[2] Clearly, organizations need to do better. And they can if they approach change with the right attitude, from the right angle, and with a solid set of action *steps*—which is what this chapter offers.

The Eight Steps

In 1995, John Kotter identified a number of steps that managers could take to create enduring change.[3] Those steps build on each other and boost the chances that a transformation effort will succeed. Kotter's eight-step process has attracted widespread attention, so we will cover it here in some detail. You can use these steps to guide companywide change efforts that you're leading, as well as changes you're initiating in your own HR department. In addition, you can coach other executives and managers throughout your firm to use these steps in order to successfully lead a change initiative. "HR in Action: Implementing the Eight Steps to Change" describes how one company used these steps to drive a broad change initiative.

Step 1: Establish a Sense of Urgency

Establishing a sense of urgency is crucial for combating complacency and gaining the cooperation you need to effect change. As Kotter explains, most successful change efforts begin when a few people or a group starts to examine changes that may mean new competitive realities for the company. These changes may take

HR in Action: Implementing the Eight Steps to Change

American Nonwovens Corporation, a Mississippi-based manufacturer of textiles, knew it had to change. With fewer than 200 employees, the company competed in the international arena against huge rivals. As Danny Avery, former Corporate Director of Administration, Quality, and Training (which encompassed HR), explains, "To survive, we needed a way to identify and standardize best practices in manufacturing. We decided that becoming ISO 9000 compliant [following a specialized methodology for standardizing and documenting best practices] would enable us to take this step."

Avery facilitated a change initiative that ultimately modeled the eight steps described by Kotter. He *established a sense of urgency* by pulling together the leadership from the company's three manufacturing facilities—"which all operated in a free-standing way"—and reinforced the seriousness of the company's competitive situation. Sensing some resistance from general manager of the Kentucky facility, which employed half of the American Nonwovens' workforce, he *formed a guiding coalition* by gaining the trust of the facility's remaining leadership.

Next the coalition *defined a compelling vision:* becoming the leading manufacturer of the specific product line offered by the company and produced in the Kentucky operation. The coalition *communicated the vision* by various means. For example, it ran company-developed slogans across scrolling marquees in the three factories. Avery himself also met frequently with shift supervisors and employees to explain the reasons behind the change effort and answer their questions. He particularly targeted opinion leaders—individuals whose names came up most frequently in hallway and shop-floor conversations.

The coalition then *empowered others to act on the vision* by identifying the six positions common to all manufacturing lines, and then asking employees, "For this particular position, who does this job better than anyone else?" The guiding team then asked the identified experts to explain exactly how they did their jobs. One chosen expert was bitter about management and nearly illiterate, but an excellent performer on the job. The simple act of asking him to share his expertise and thus become part of the "core team," Avery says, made this employee enormously proud. He promptly committed to the ISO initiative.

Similar examples of employees' coming on board and contributing to the documentation of best practices constituted the change initiative's *short-term wins*. The company *consolidated these gains* by basing training on the finalized instructions for how to perform key processes. Several documented processes also generated ideas for product improvements and new applications of products (which include everything from roofing tiles to feminine-hygiene products). Finally, American Nonwovens *institutionalized the new approaches* by standardizing the identified best practices using the ISO 9000 framework.

This change initiative, which unfolded over six months in the mid-1990s, generated impressive results. In addition to the new-product ideas, the company saw improvements in employee morale and pride. "There was an *esprit de corps* that we hadn't seen before," Avery says. "No one had ever asked employees what *they* thought about their work." The adversarial quality of the relationship between corporate and local management also evaporated, and customers praised the new consistency they saw in the company's products.

SOURCE: Danny Avery, telephone conversation with author, December 16, 2003.

numerous forms—demographic shifts that signal the need for new hiring strategies or HR policies, technological advances, changes in market position, and so forth.

If you've identified such a change, you need to get the word out that crisis is imminent—or that great opportunities await if the company seizes them in time. Creating this sense of urgency is essential, because merely launching a transformation program depends on the energetic cooperation of many individuals. Without a sense of urgency, people won't step up to the plate—and the effort fizzles.

But conveying urgency can prove surprisingly difficult. Why? People don't like to be driven out of their comfort zones. Executives sometimes overestimate the degree of urgency they've created. And managers may lack the patience to lay this critical foundation for the change process. Finally, some leaders become paralyzed by the fear that morale will drop throughout the company, that stock price will sink, or that they'll be blamed for creating a crisis.

Change leaders must move beyond these fears and other pitfalls. They need to encourage a frank discussion throughout the company of the signs they've detected that, if left unaddressed, may hamper the company's ability to compete. If you sense a strong "shoot the messenger" sentiment in the company, consider bringing in someone from outside to deliver the painful news. For instance, suppose you've analyzed salary ranges for specific job descriptions and have seen a sharp rise in certain types of roles, and you expect to get resistance to a proposal to raise salaries from the other members of the executive team. In this case, you may want to bring in an outside analyst to shed additional light on the situation and provide insights on how the company can best continue to attract the most valuable employees. Your goal? To make current conditions seem more perilous than venturing into the unknown. In fact, some executives deliberately manufacture a crisis to jump-start the change process—for example, commissioning an employee-attitude survey that they know will bring back terrible results, and then publishing the findings throughout the company. (See also "Create a Sense of Urgency by Finding Gaps".)

Create a Sense of Urgency by Finding Gaps

To feel a sense of urgency, people need to understand the differences between their company's current conditions and a desired future. By determining what is critical to the success of the organization in each of its core processes—for example, hiring and retention, marketing, manufacturing, satisfying clients—and by detailing the desired future states, managers have an opportunity to identify any "gaps" in organizational performance. These gaps can be the basis for broad-based motivation to change.

Xerox Discovers a Critical Cost Gap

In 1979, Xerox's copier division set out to benchmark its productivity measures against those of rising foreign competitors. Xerox had invented the copier industry, and virtually owned it until this time. But now Japanese companies were coming out with smaller, less expensive, and more reliable models. Xerox was aware of a substantial cost difference between its operations and those of these new competitors, but lacked the details.

Working through its Japanese partner, Fuji Xerox, the American company performed *gap analysis* to identify and measure what turned out to be a shocking cost gap. Its Japanese rivals were profitably selling their machines in the United States at less than Xerox's own cost of production! This was startling news. Once the gap was quantified, it became the centerpiece of a change initiative that introduced the quality and benchmarking techniques that successfully reformed Xerox.

How to tell if the urgency in your company is sufficiently intense? Kotter says that when about 75 percent of a company's managers feel convinced that the status quo is no longer acceptable, the company is experiencing considerable urgency.

Step 2: Create a Guiding Coalition

Once people throughout an organization feel a sense of urgency, leaders must create a powerful, guiding coalition to sustain that urgency and orchestrate the rest of the change process. Whether this coalition consists of five, fifteen, or fifty people, its members need to have significant credibility and authority. These qualities can come from formal sources such as a person's job title—and from less formal sources, including expertise, reputation, and relationships inside and outside the company.

Most effective guiding coalitions comprise senior managers as well as people from outside that managerial core—such as board members, someone representing a major customer, employees from various levels within the company, or a respected union leader. For instance, if you're leading a new initiative aimed at reducing turnover at your firm, you might want to build a guiding coalition consisting of yourself, several managers of departments that are experiencing the most turnover of employees, a customer representative who can speak to the problems that his firm experiences owing to rapid turnover of your firm's employees, and maybe even former employees who are willing to share their reasons for wanting to leave the company. The presence of people from outside the normal hierarchy may create some awkwardness, but it's necessary. Why? It signals the urgent fact that the existing hierarchy isn't working. "Outsiders" can bring valuable insights, expectations, and ideas.

Once a guiding coalition is established, the group needs to arrive at a shared understanding of the company's problems and opportunities and begin building some degree of trust and communication. Many guiding coalitions use a series of off-site retreats to accomplish these tasks.

Step 3: Develop a Compelling Vision

People in charge of change must develop a clear vision of a new and better future. An effective vision can get most employees on the side of change. But what constitutes an effective vision? John Kotter has suggested six characteristics. From his perspective, an effective vision comprises the following characteristics:[4]

- **Describes a desirable future.** The outcome is one that people would be happy to have right now if they could;

- **Is compelling.** It describes a future so much better than the current reality that people will gladly undertake the effort and sacrifice as necessary to attain it;

- **Is realistic.** People perceive it as within their grasp with some hard work;

- **Is focused.** It limits itself to a manageable and coherent set of goals, such as Six Sigma quality, or customer service that resolves a customer's problem with a single phone call;

- **Is flexible.** It can adapt to changing circumstances; and

- **Is easy to communicate.** Employees at different levels can readily understand it.

Concision is another quality of a good vision: If you can't describe your vision to someone else in under five minutes *and* capture his or her attention, your vision will likely fall flat. What might a vision that has all these qualities look like? Here's one example:

> *We want to reduce our costs by at least 30 percent and increase the speed with which we can respond to customers by at least 40 percent. In three years, we will have leapfrogged our biggest competitors and reaped all the benefits: better satisfied customers, increased revenue growth, more job security, and enormous pride.*[5]

As another illustration, let's again consider the example of an initiative you've decided to lead that will aim to reduce turnover in the company. In this case, your vision for the change effort may be something like "We want to decrease turnover by 10 percent by the end of next year and become known as one of the ten best companies to work for in our region and industry."

To make a vision compelling, leaders must also "live" the vision—that is, demonstrate the values, focus, and dedication required to turn the vision into reality. It's not enough to just define and communicate a vision: You and the other leaders must sincerely believe in it yourselves and commit to it wholeheartedly.

Who creates the vision for a change initiative, and how does the process unfold? The whole thing takes time and patience, and can be quite messy. Often a single person provides the first draft. Then the guiding coalition and other individuals model and revise the draft. It can feel like "one step forward, two steps back," and the combination of analytical thinking and dreaming can seem confusing. For many companies striving to create a corporatewide vision, the process can take months or even longer.

Step 4: Communicate the Vision

Once change leaders have developed an effective vision, they must communicate that vision to others in ways that make the benefits of change clear. They must be very specific about: (1) how the change will improve the business (through greater employee satisfaction, customer service, product quality, sales revenues, productivity, or some other measure), and (2) how those improvements will benefit people throughout the firm. These benefits might include higher pay, larger bonuses, new opportunities for advancement, or greater job security.

Price Pritchett, a change management expert at Dallas-based Pritchett & Associates, says that 20 percent of employees tend to support a change from the start, another 50 percent are "fence-sitters," and the remaining 30 percent tend to oppose the change. Fence-sitters and resisters must be converted and then enlisted to participate in realizing the vision. It isn't enough to just identify the problem and agree on how to proceed. You have to get people excited and involved.

That means constant and widespread communication of the vision. In the most successful transformation efforts, managers use every existing communication channel to spread the word of the vision. They write lively articles about the vision in company newsletters, discuss vision and transformation at monthly and quarterly meetings, and arrange for people to take courses focusing on business problems and the new vision. Even more important, they seek to embody the vision—to "walk the talk." When other managers and employees see a consistency between your words and deeds, they become far more likely to support the vision you've described to them.

Two cautions about the "vision." First, for the vision to be inspiring and motivational, managers and employees must be able to translate it into actions that will produce tangible results. So in communicating a vision, always explain what *specifically* this vision will produce. It might be a 25 percent reduction in employee turnover, a 20 percent profit improvement next year, or a hiring decision in one day instead of three. Whatever it is for your organization, don't allow a lofty vision to crowd out specific improvement goals. Second, ensure that the vision you're communicating is compatible with the company's core values—those values that have sustained it over the years. If a vision does not resonate with those values, people may feel confused about what's most important to do.

Step 5: Empower Others to Act on the Vision

A sense of urgency, a guiding coalition, and a compelling vision communicated effectively all help to encourage people to act on the vision. But to further empower people to support change, you must also remove obstacles to acting on the vision. These obstacles can take several forms:

- Narrow job categories that undermine employees' efforts to boost productivity, think about the company from the customer's viewpoint, or effect other changes essential to carrying out the vision

- Compensation or performance-appraisal systems that force people to choose between the vision and their own self-interest

- Supervisors who make demands that conflict with the overall change effort

Whatever the obstacle, you need to remove it if your change effort has any hopes of succeeding. No change leader can eliminate every obstacle, but the largest ones should be confronted and taken out of the picture. Kotter notes that if an obstacle is a person, the company may well need to sever its relationship with him or her. In such cases, the firm must treat the person fairly and in a way that reflects the vision and the organization's core values.

Step 6: Generate Short-Term Wins

Successful, enduring change takes time. When people realize that, many become discouraged or disappointed, and their sense of urgency withers away. To keep urgency levels up, deliberately create the conditions that will enable people to score short-term wins. Such early successes need to come within one or two years of the launch of a major transformation effort. For example, if you're striving to realize a vision of your firm becoming one of the top ten best companies to work for in your region or industry, early wins might take several forms, including:

- High employee-satisfaction ratings

- A leveling off of turnover in one or two departments

- A positive article about your company published in an industry or trade journal

The key is to *actively look* for opportunities to score early wins—and then to celebrate the success and reward the people involved. One company selected an employee-attitudes survey initiative six months into a transformation effort because staff members could design and launch it relatively quickly, a small team of people devoted to the new vision could handle the project, and the team could work on the project outside the established departmental structure without interference. The project's success enhanced the turnover-reduction change effort's credibility.

Step 7: Consolidate Gains and Produce More Change

Though it's essential to plan for, create, and celebrate short-term wins, resist any urge to declare victory too soon. Until changes have been embedded in a company's culture—which Kotter maintains can take as long as five or ten years—new ways of working remain vulnerable to regression. A premature victory celebration kills momentum. Why? People who have been resisting the transformation effort see a declaration of victory as an opportunity to stop change. And once momentum dies out, the powerful forces of tradition take over—reversing all the progress the company has made.

Instead of declaring victory after an important short-term win, use the credibility those early successes generate to tackle even bigger problems. For instance, if your turnover-reduction change initiative has led to a leveling off of turnover in a key department in your firm, examine ways to address high-turnover problems in several other important functions. Confront additional systems and structures that conflict with the vision. To illustrate, consider establishing a new exit-interview system that generates more useful information about what causes turnover among specific categories of jobs or particular demographic groups of employees. Ensure that new hires, promotions, and professional-development programs align behind the vision. Take on large components of the overall transformation effort.

Through it all, maintain the long view. Realize that during the years over which the transformation effort unfolds, the biggest changes may not come until five or so years into the project. By consolidating gains and using them to produce even more change, you build further momentum.

Step 8: Anchor New Approaches in the Company's Culture

Getting an organization to change requires risk-taking and effort by many people. So once you've achieved your objective, the last thing you want is for all those hard-earned gains to slip away. And they will, if you don't take steps to embed new ways of doing work in the company's culture. You can consolidate and cement gains through (1) policies that describe how work is to be done, (2) information systems, and (3) new reporting relationships. For example, once it had achieved a key goal—over 99 percent on-time deliveries of furniture orders—SQA, Herman Miller's low-cost office-furniture unit, institutionalized its gains through a performance measurement system that kept everyone's focus on that metric.[6] All managers and employees in the production facility, from top to bottom, were expected to know the current level of on-time delivery. Moreover, the company's executive team tied various rewards to performance on that metric. If you've succeeded in achieving your vision of seeing your firm become one of the best organizations to work for in your region or industry, you might secure that success in several ways. To illustrate, perhaps you could design a new HR policy that requires managers to gather and interpret information on employee problems more frequently and thoroughly than they did before.

To follow through on the change process, managers and employees throughout an organization must be as concerned with institutionalizing the "journey" as with implementing a new process itself. The ultimate goal? *Continuous* improvement. How can change leaders ensure that successful new approaches become "the way we do things around here"? The key is to root new behaviors in social norms and shared values. Kotter recommends several particularly effective strategies:

- **Prove it.** Show people how the new approaches, behaviors, and attitudes have improved the company's performance. Use every opportunity to communicate the connection between change and its payoffs. Bring up the subject during meetings; run articles in the company newsletter showing how changes have yielded specific, measurable, and positive results that benefit everyone. For instance, an article about how reductions in employee turnover have boosted sales revenues—which has helped to pull the company out of a financial slump and make everyone's jobs more secure—will inspire managers and employees alike.

- **Plan for succession.** Ensure that as top managers retire, their successors continue to champion the changes the company has achieved. If necessary, redefine requirements for promotion so that successors understand the importance of sustaining the benefits reaped from the transformation effort. With promotion to or hiring into topmost positions, it's vital that the board of directors understands the transformation initiative in some detail, so members can ensure the right fit between newly appointed executives and the company's long-term transformation goals.

To assess your organization's approach to change based on the eight steps outlined in this section, see assessment tool 5-1.

Leaders and Managers: Roles for HR Professionals

HR professionals, along with other leaders and managers at all levels in an organization, play central roles in the eight-step change process. Among many other responsibilities as change managers, they

- help institutionalize successful change through employee development, rewards, and organizational design;

- facilitate meetings and off-site conferences among managers to devise plans for implementing change initiatives;

- hire and assign consultants to projects related to a change effort;

- reassign and/or outplace personnel displaced by change; and

- design and arrange for executive, managerial, and employee training needed to secure the successes of a transformation.

Assessment Tool 5-1
Your Organization and the Eight-Step
Change Process

Now that you are acquainted with the eight steps of successful change, do a little diagnosis of your own organization. Consider how it has approached change in the past and how it is approaching any current initiatives. Then score it using this brief diagnostic test, using a 1–5 scale ("1" indicates "strongly disagree"; "5" indicates "strongly agree").

1. Establishes a sense of urgency for change

    1   2   3   4   5

2. Has a powerful guiding coalition to lead major change efforts

    1   2   3   4   5

3. Has a compelling vision

    1   2   3   4   5

More important, HR professionals can serve as both managers and leaders in guiding change. How? Leaders create an appealing vision of the future and then develop a logical strategy for making it a reality. They also motivate people to pursue the vision, even in the face of obstacles. Managers, on the other hand, have the job of making complex tasks run smoothly. They have to work out the implementation details, round up the required resources, and keep employee energy channeled in the right direction. While leaders create a vision and plan for extending the train tracks into new territory, managers get the tracks built and make sure that the trains run on time. Thus, it is clear why the eight steps of change outlined here require effective leaders *and* managers, at all levels of the organization.

4. Communicates its vision effectively

   1   2   3   4   5

5. Empowers people to act on the vision

   1   2   3   4   5

6. Plans for, creates, and rewards short-term wins for each change initiative

   1   2   3   4   5

7. Consolidates gains to produce additional change

   1   2   3   4   5

8. Embeds new behaviors, attitudes, and values in the company's culture

   1   2   3   4   5

How does your organization fare on these parameters? A score of 3 or lower in any category points to serious weaknesses that you'll want to identify and correct.

How will you serve as both leader and manager in a change initiative at your firm? Identify what you need to do to fulfill the role of leader—such as creating and realizing a compelling vision and motivating others to turn the vision into reality. Also identify what you need to do to fulfill the role of manager—including figuring out precisely how various components of the change initiative will be carried out, what resources the effort will require and how they'll be obtained, and how you'll ensure that managers and employees throughout the company will remain energized by and focused on the transformation effort. If you feel uncertain about some aspects of these two roles, decide how you'll get help with those areas. For example, hire a communications consultant if you need help designing a comprehensive communication plan that will keep your firm's workforce informed of progress and challenges related to the change effort.

In practice, of course, the distinction between leaders and managers is fuzzy and often arbitrary. An effective leader always needs managerial skills, and every competent manager provides leadership to his or her direct reports. To evaluate your own effectiveness as a leader, it might be helpful to take the self-diagnostic test found in appendix A.

John Kotter has described the relationship of leadership and management in a simple two-by-two matrix, shown in figure 5-1. The diagram suggests that transformation goes nowhere when both leadership and management are lacking. Good short-term results are feasible when *either* effective leadership *or* effective managers are involved. But for a company to enjoy long-term transformation success, both must be present, as in the figure.

FIGURE 5-1

The Relationship of Leadership and Management

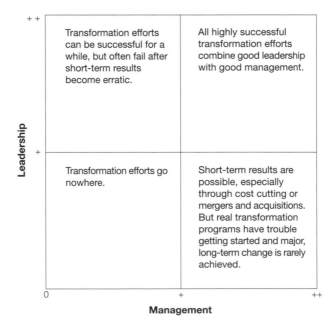

Transformation efforts can be successful for a while, but often fail after short-term results become erratic.	All highly successful transformation efforts combine good leadership with good management.
Transformation efforts go nowhere.	Short-term results are possible, especially through cost cutting or mergers and acquisitions. But real transformation programs have trouble getting started and major, long-term change is rarely achieved.

Source: John P. Kotter, *Leading Change* (Boston: Harvard Business School Press, 1996), 129.

HR professionals must understand their unique role in a change process and collaborate with other leaders and managers if the transformation efforts they're guiding are to succeed in the short *and* long run. In addition, they must recognize the critical role of rank and file employees, who need to actively participate throughout the change effort. And they need to recognize as well the traps that may prevent successful change. (See "Common Pitfalls of Change Management" below.)

Summing Up

This chapter presented eight steps for creating change. They are:

Step 1. Establish a sense of urgency.

Step 2. Create a powerful guiding coalition.

Step 3. Develop a compelling vision.

Step 4. Communicate the vision.

Step 5. Empower others to act on the vision.

Step 6. Generate short-term wins.

Step 7. Consolidate gains and push for more change.

Step 8. Anchor new approaches in the company's culture.

The chapter also explored HR professionals' dual role as leaders and managers—and the importance of having enough of both during a major transformation effort.

Leveraging Chapter Insights: Critical Questions

- Does your organization implement the eight-step change model described in this chapter? If so, what have been the results? If not, which steps are missing from the company's

Common Pitfalls of Change Management

When your organization is going through a transformation process, in addition to following Kotter's advice for driving the eight-step change process, watch for the following common pitfalls to managing change:

- **Don't try to impose a canned solution developed somewhere else.** Instead, develop the solution within the unit that most needs change.

- **Don't place your bets on a companywide solution driven from the top.** In some instances, this has worked—but usually only in cases where the company was heading down the tubes and everyone knew it. If the company is large, the odds of changing an entire business in a single masterstroke are slim. Make the solution specific to the unit or units that need change.

- **Don't bank on a technical fix alone.** Businesses are social systems, not machines. To be effective, a technical fix must fit comfortably within the social fabric of the workplace, otherwise the workplace's immune system will attack it. Technical solutions usually miss the root causes of problems and fail to deal with the attitudes, skills, and motivations associated with them. In one classic case, a mining company's engineering solution to production efficiency was technically superior, but inadvertently broke up employee groups that had learned to work together and to support each other in a dangerous environment. The miners resisted the technical solution because it failed to account for how they worked together.

- **Don't attempt to change everything at once.** The biggest error of top-driven programmatic change is that it tries to do too much at once. Unless the entire organization is in crisis, begin change at the periphery, in units far from corporate headquarters, where local managers and their people can run the show and maintain control. That's what happened at Herman Miller, where the substantive change initially took place in its small operating unit, SQA. It's unlikely that the same success would have been achieved had Herman Miller tried to change everything in every one of its operating units in a bold stroke.

approach to change? For example, is the company's vision unclear or not sufficiently compelling? Instead of consolidating early wins and using them to build further momentum for change, does your company declare victory too soon? Do new approaches get "put on the shelf" instead of being woven into the company's culture?

- What steps might *you* take to strengthen your company's performance on the eight-step change process?

- In what ways do you serve as a leader in your organization? In what ways do you serve as a manager?

CHAPTER SIX

Implementation

Putting Your Change Plans in Motion

Key Topics Covered in This Chapter

- *How to enlist the support and involvement of key people in a change initiative*

- *The importance of relentless communication*

- *The importance of supporting the plan with consistent behaviors*

- *How to develop enabling structures (i.e., training, pilot programs, and a reward system)*

- *Ways to create results-driven change*

- *Ways to celebrate milestones*

- *The role of consultants*

Y OU'VE CONVINCED people in your department, division, or organization that change is necessary, and that the change vision is the right one. Now it's time to move forward with implementing the change. As you might imagine, implementation rarely proceeds smoothly. As soon as people get into the nitty-gritty of putting their change initiative into action, they discover that there is no tidy, step-by-step march to the envisioned future. People make mistakes. External factors upset schedules. Key people quit or get transferred. Different groups forget to communicate with each other.

A survey identified seven implementation problems that occurred in at least 60 percent of the ninety-three firms polled:[1]

1. Implementation took more time than originally allocated (76 percent).

2. Major problems surfaced during implementation that had not been identified beforehand (74 percent).

3. Coordination of implementation activities (for example, task forces or committees) was not effective enough (66 percent).

4. Competing activities and crises distracted attention from implementing this strategic decision (64 percent).

5. Capabilities (skill and abilities) of employees involved with the implementation were not sufficient (63 percent).

6. Training and instruction given to lower-level employees were not adequate (62 percent).

7. Uncontrollable factors in the external environment had an adverse impact on implementation (60 percent).

Other implementation problems include insufficient support for change or unclear goals. Although implementation can pose daunting challenges, you can improve the odds of success if you enlist the support and involvement of key people, craft a solid plan, communicate relentlessly about the change effort, support the implementation plan with consistent behaviors, develop enabling structures, and celebrate milestone successes. As an HR professional leading *or* facilitating a change initiative in your firm, you may find yourself playing key roles in any of these aspects of implementation. These roles may include inviting input from peer executives or managers to craft a plan, developing a communications program about the change effort, designing enabling structures such as training and reward programs, creating systems for celebrating victories, and other responsibilities.

Enlist the Support and Involvement of Key People

Implementation of a change effort you're leading will go more smoothly if it has the backing and involvement of key people—not just the CEO and his or her court. You also need to enlist other executives, managers, and employees whom others respect; individuals with key technical skills, people with access to vital resources, and the informal leaders to whom people naturally turn for direction and advice. For example, suppose you're leading an initiative to improve succession planning throughout your company's executive and managerial ranks. You might want your implementation team to include not only executives and managers but also employees who can shed light on who might make valuable successors to departing or promoted managers. In addition, you'd want input from people who can help you devise or enhance systems for collecting and interpreting performance data and documenting success plan decisions. You might also want to engage the participation of external consultants who specialize in succession management or representatives from companies in other, noncompeting industries who can share what they've learned from their own experiences.

So how can you pinpoint these potential implementation team members? Authors Michael Tushman and Charles O'Reilly offer this advice:

> To determine who these key individuals are and what their responses to the change might be, ask: Who has the power to make or break the change? Who controls critical resources or expertise? Then think through how the change will likely affect each of these individuals and how each is likely to react toward the change. Who will gain or lose something. . . . Are there blocs of individuals likely to mobilize against or in support of the change effort?[2]

Enlisting support entails building an effective team of change makers who can act together toward stated goals. But how can you be sure you've picked the right people for the team? See assessment tool 6-1 to find out.

When you're building your team, keep in mind that it's also important to avoid enlisting people who may hamper or even derail the change effort. (See "Tips on Who Should *Not* Be on the Change Implementation Team.")

Craft an Implementation Plan

While a vision may guide and inspire implementation team members during the change process, people in your organization also need a nuts-and-bolts plan for what to do, and when and how to do it. For instance, a change initiative centered on better succession management may include a study of succession management practices in your industry, among many other components. Your implementation plan would need to include details about each aspect of the initiative. To illustrate, who will be responsible for the succession management study? When will they aim to complete the study? How much it will cost, and what resources will be called on (consultants? internal teams?) to conduct the study?

Assessment Tool 6-1
Pick the Right Change Team

Answer each of the following questions with "Yes" or "No."

1. Are enough of your company's *key players* (people in relevant positions of power) members of the team?

   Yes   No

2. Do team members have the relevant *expertise* to do the job and make intelligent decisions?

   Yes   No

3. Does the team include the needed *range* of perspectives and disciplines to do the job and make intelligent decisions?

   Yes   No

4. Does the team include people with *sufficient credibility* so that employees and management will treat its members' decisions seriously?

   Yes   No

5. Does the team include people with demonstrated *leadership skills*?

   Yes   No

6. Are the team members capable of forgoing personal immediate interests in favor of the *larger organizational goal*?

   Yes   No

If you answered "yes" to most of these questions, the team guiding the change effort is strong and in a good position to succeed. If you answered "no" to any questions, it might be a good idea to revisit your team choices. (For more on selecting team members, see "Tips on Who Should Not Be on the Team.")

SOURCE: John F. Kotter, *Leading Change* (Boston: Harvard Business School Press, 1996).

Tips on *Who Should* Not *Be on the* Change Implementation Team

In his book *Leading Change,* John Kotter recommends keeping three types of people off your team:

1. **People with big egos.** Big egos fill the room, leaving little or no space for anybody else to participate in or contribute to change. People with big egos don't always understand their own limitations or ways in which others' strengths can complement those limitations.

2. **"Snakes."** A "snake" is the kind of person who secretly poisons relationships between team members. He or she is "an expert at telling Sally something about Fred and Fred something about Sally that undermines Sally and Fred's relationship."

3. **Reluctant players.** These are people who lack the time or enthusiasm to provide energy to the team. However, keeping such players off your team may be difficult, because some reluctant players may have the expertise and/or organizational power you need.

SOURCE: John P. Kotter, *Leading Change* (Boston: Harvard Business School Press, 1996), 59–61.

Your implementation plan should map out the entire effort—specifying everything from where the first meetings should be held to the date by which the company should reasonably expect to achieve its change goals. Here are some characteristics of a good implementation plan:[3]

- **It's simple.** An overly complex plan may confuse and frustrate participants in the change effort. So if your flowchart of activities and milestones looks like the wiring diagram for the space shuttle, rethink it with an eye toward simplicity and coherence.

- **It's created by people at all affected levels.** Your implementation plan is part of the solution, and shouldn't be imposed on the people asked to push it forward. If implementers and other people affected by the change actively participate in making the plan, they'll feel more enthusiastic about supporting the initiative once it's rolled into action. Remember, too, that a plan devised solely by strategists is less likely to reflect the realities of the business and the organization's potential accomplishments than a plan built on the ideas of employees from all levels.

- **It's structured in achievable chunks.** Overly ambitious plans are usually doomed to failure. People look at them and say, "We'll never get this done—not in our lifetimes." They'll feel defeated from the beginning. So build a plan that people can tackle in manageable, achievable segments.

- **It specifies roles and responsibilities.** Like every endeavor, a change plan should clearly detail the roles and responsibilities of everyone involved. Every planned outcome should be the acknowledged responsibility of one or more individuals. Those individuals should publicly state that they welcome and accept the responsibility. Input from all levels of the organization will help to achieve this role-oriented focus.

- **It's flexible.** Not surprisingly, change programs seldom follow their planned trajectories or timetables. Thus, a good implementation plan is a living document open to revision. Organizations that lock themselves into rigid schedules, goals, and events ultimately find themselves detached from the shifts occurring in the world around them.

Communicate Relentlessly

Consistent, ongoing communication can motivate managers and employees, help them overcome resistance to an initiative, prepare people for the pluses and minuses of change, and give people a personal stake in the process. Effective communication can set the tone for a change program and is critical to implementation from the very start. But don't rely on a single Big Bang announcement to keep people aligned behind the effort. Communication must be ongoing. (See "HR in Action: Putting Communication to Work" for a story emphasizing the importance of ongoing communication.) Here are ten tips for communicating during a change effort:[4]

1. **Specify the nature of the change.** Slogans, themes, and phrases don't define what the change is expected to achieve. Communicate specific information about how the change will affect customer satisfaction, quality, market share or sales, or productivity. For example, with your succession management initiative, let people know that a good succession management program enables your company to develop a deep, varied pool of talented individuals who can better serve the organization's needs in an ever-changing and uncertain future. It can also improve retention because it puts skilled people into leadership development programs, strengthening their awareness of and commitment to their professional path.[5]

2. **Explain why.** People throughout an organization are often left in the dark about the business reasons behind the change. You may have spent lots of time studying the problem and digging out the facts, but your peers and their direct reports may not necessarily be privy to that same information. In addition to specifying the nature and benefits of the change, share with people the various options available and why some (or one) are better than the others.

3. **Explain the scope of the change, even if it contains bad news.** Some people are more affected by change projects than others. And that leads to lots of fear-generating speculation. Fear and uncertainty can paralyze people and entire companies. You can short-circuit fear and uncertainty with the facts. But don't sugarcoat them. For example, if a cost-cutting or strategic-refocusing change initiative will involve layoffs, be

HR in Action:
Putting Communication to Work

Communication played a big role in the successful change program that pulled Continental Airlines out of a nosedive in the 1990s. Here's how president and CEO Greg Brenneman described Continental's approach in an article for the *Harvard Business Review*:

> *When I arrived at Continental, it was a mean and lousy place to work. For years, different groups of employees had been pitted against one another in the effort to drive down labor costs. Management's implicit communication policy had been, "Don't tell anybody anything unless absolutely required." As a result, most employees learned of the company's activities, plans, and performance through the press. Talk about sending a message about who matters and who doesn't.*
>
> *On top of that, employees had no place to go with ideas or questions. There were forms for employees' suggestions on how to improve the operations, but the suggestions disappeared into a black hole. Add to that the fact that corporate headquarters was locked up like Fort Knox: The president's secretary had a buzzer under her desk that she could use to summon the police.*
>
> *Needless to say, morale was terrible. A couple of weeks after I arrived, I was walking the ramp in Houston saying hello to our mechanics and baggage handlers, and helping to throw a bag or two, when I noticed that almost all the employees had torn the Continental logos from their shirts. When I asked one mechanic why he had done this, he explained, "When I go to Wal-Mart tonight, I don't want anyone to know that I work for Continental." His response still sends chills down my spine.*
>
> *Now, how to create a new culture is the topic of hundreds, if not thousands, of books and articles. But Gordon [Bethune] and I didn't bother with them. We agreed that a healthy culture is*

Continued

simply a function of several factors, namely: honesty, trust, dignity, and respect. They all go together; they reinforce one another. When they are constants in a business, people become engaged in their work. They care; they talk; they laugh. And then fun happens pretty naturally. But honesty and the rest don't just sprout up like weeds in a cornfield, especially when there has been a long drought. In a turnaround situation, people are tense and suspicious for good reason. They've been lied to. They've seen their friends get fired. They fear they will be next.

So cultivating honesty, trust, dignity, and respect becomes the job of the leaders. It may even be their most important job; Gordon and I certainly considered it our top priority. That's why when we took over, we started talking with employees at every opportunity. We got out there in the airports and on the planes. We loaded bags; we stood alongside the agents at ticket counters. We just talked at every opportunity about our plans for the airline and how we were going to accomplish them. In general, our communication policy changed from, "Don't tell anybody anything unless absolutely required," to "Tell everybody everything."

SOURCE: Greg Brenneman, "Right Away and All at Once: How We Saved Continental," *Harvard Business Review* (September–October 1998): 176.

up front about it. To help anchor people, also explain the things that will *not* change—such as the company's commitment to its core values, its focus on a particular market, and so forth.

4. **Develop a graphic representation of the change project that people can understand and hold in their heads.** This graphic representation might consist of a flowchart depicting what must happen for the initiative to succeed. Or it may be an image of what the changed enterprise will look like once the initiative has been implemented. Whatever representation you decide to use, keep it clear, simple, and memorable.

5. **Predict negative aspects of implementation.** There are bound to be negatives, so help people anticipate them. For

instance, a change effort involving blending and restructuring of several departments might bring confusion and chaos for a while, as the people involved master new reporting relationships or job responsibilities. Be up front about the more challenging aspects of your initiative rather than trying to sugarcoat them. And let people know that you have every confidence that they can handle the challenges.

6. **Explain the criteria for success and how it will be measured.** Define success clearly, and devise metrics for progress toward it. If you fail to establish clear measures for what you aim to accomplish, how will anyone know when they've moved forward? Measure progress as you move forward—and then communicate that progress. For instance, clarify how you'll measure your succession management effort's progress toward achieving your company's diversity goals, and decide how you'll get the word out about that progress.

7. **Explain how people will be rewarded for success.** People need incentive for the added work and disruptions that change requires. Be very clear about how individuals will be rewarded for progress toward change goals. Will they receive bonuses? The ability to work more flexible hours? Recognition in the company newsletter or at the end-of-year awards banquet? Dinner for high-performance teams at a special restaurant?

8. **Repeat, repeat, and repeat the purpose of change and actions planned.** If the initial announcement doesn't generate questions, do not assume that people in your organization have accepted the need for change. They may simply be surprised, puzzled, or shocked by the prospect of the initiative. So follow up your initial announcement meeting with another meeting. Then follow that meeting with communications that address individual aspects of the change project.

9. **Use a diverse set of communication styles appropriate for your audience.** Successful change programs build communications into their plans, using dedicated newsletters, events,

e-mails, and stand-up presentations to keep people informed, involved, and keyed up. These communications should be honest about successes and failures. If people lose trust in what they are hearing or reading, they will tune you out.

10. **Make communication a two-way proposition.** Remember: This is a shared enterprise. So, whenever you're leading a major change effort, spend at least as much time listening to others as you do telling them about the initiative. Listening will help keep others involved and motivated. It will also give you the feedback you need to fine-tune your implementation so that it remains on track. Those hardworking implementers you've enlisted need opportunities to share their learning and concerns with leaders who listen.

Support Your Implementation Plan with Consistent Behaviors and Messages

Once you or other change leaders in your company have articulated the need for change convincingly, enlisted broad support, crafted an implementation plan, and begun communicating relentlessly about the change, maintain that momentum by modeling and encouraging consistent behaviors and messages. Remember: When you (or any other executive or manager) are leading a change, people have their eyes on you. They listen to your words, but also look for inconsistencies between your words and what you communicate through body language and behavior. Do you and other managers throughout your firm speak and act with genuine enthusiasm for the change? Do your tone and manner signal confidence in the project, or do you appear to be going through the motions? Try to see yourself as others see you. Then make any adjustments necessary to ensure consistency in the many different channels through which you express your attitudes toward and the intentions of the change initiative. Inconsistency will send a damaging message: that management isn't serious about implementing change, or that managers are unwilling to do their part in ensuring the effort's success.

Consider this example: Not many years ago, one of the American Big Three automakers underwent a painful restructuring. Everyone was asked to sacrifice by giving up benefits today in order to achieve greater competitiveness and prosperity tomorrow. Thousands of middle managers and employees were laid off, and the company's union was asked to forgo pay and benefit increases. Because the company had made a convincing case for change, people got the message and tightened their belts; even the unions pitched in. Within months, however, senior management awarded itself and other key people bonuses and substantial pay increases. Once that inconsistent behavior became public, the bonds of trust between management and the rank and file—and their unions—broke. Collaboration turned to open hostility that simmered for nearly ten years.

At about the same time, a company in another industry was likewise supporting a belt-tightening and restructuring program. But this one did so with highly visible and consistent deeds. Its CEO set the pace by selling the corporation's three jets and taking commercial flights on his travels—in coach class, to boot. And no more limos met him at the airport. "I don't mind taking a cab," he told the business press. "They can get me to where I'm going just as fast." The company's other traveling executives followed their boss's lead. People noticed—and felt more willing to make their own sacrifices.

Which of these companies do you suppose built the most support for its change program?

The story of SQA, Herman Miller's successful low-cost office furniture unit, offers additional lessons about the importance of consistency. The company used a consistent set of messages to support its effort to increase on-time, accurate fulfillment of orders. Everyone understood that this was the unit's key measure of successful change. So SQA managers came up with several ways to reinforce that understanding. For example, they installed signboards at every entrance to the plant, and each morning they posted the previous day's percentage of on-time orders. No one could enter or leave the plant without knowing the previous day's performance. Managers also added the on-time order metric to internal e-mail messages. "Yesterday's percentage of on-time accurately filled orders was 99.2 percent." The vice president of operations even adopted the practice of randomly asking employees if they knew the previous day's score. A correct answer was rewarded with either a crisp $100 bill or a paid day off.

What messages or behaviors would be consistent with the change program that *you're* leading or facilitating?

Develop Enabling Structures

Enabling structures are the activities and programs needed to underpin any successful change-implementation effort. Such structures usually include pilot programs, training, reward systems, and employee-retention and outplacement programs—areas where HR professionals bring their most important talents and expertise.

- **Pilot programs.** These programs give people opportunities to grapple with implementation and its problems on a smaller, more manageable scale. Pilots are test beds in which implementers can experiment with and "debug" change initiatives before rolling them out more broadly. These programs can be valuable proving grounds, since it's almost always easier and less risky to change a single department than an entire company. For example, if you're leading an effort to adopt a new performance-management methodology in your company, you might design a pilot program that enables managers and employees in one department to experiment with the methodology and offer suggestions for using it most effectively.

- **Training programs.** Motorola and General Electric developed formal training programs that served as key enablers for their ensuing quality initiatives. Xerox did the same when it set up its companywide benchmarking program in the mid-1980s.

Every Xerox employee received a copy of "the little yellow book," as they called the company's how-to manual on benchmarking methods. Moreover, skilled trainers were placed in almost every operating unit of the company. If you're designing training programs for a change effort that you're leading or facilitating, you may end up deciding to have consultants initially supply the training—with the ultimate goal of having managers or employees conduct training once they've mastered the new process or methodology.

- **Reward systems.** People generally adopt behaviors that produce rewards, while abandoning those that go unrewarded. Thus, if your change program asks people to work harder, work smarter, or work in new ways, you'll need to design a reward system that aligns with the desired behaviors. However, as you well know, the details and pitfalls of crafting incentive programs are complex and differ across organizations. Thus you need to convey to other executives and managers the importance of designing these programs within the unique context of your organization.

- **Employee-retention programs.** No change effort can be implemented successfully unless companies retain those employees who are most committed to the initiative and who have the skills most valuable to the effort. There are lots of ways to improve retention. For example, consider offering an internal degree program to reduce turnover of needed technical specialists. Encourages managers throughout your firm to give employees positive reinforcement, describe strategies for doing so, and explain the benefits of such treatment. Specifically, direct reports who receive positive reinforcement will be more likely to stay *and* voice their satisfaction with the company and their bosses to friends and family—which can serve as a strong recruitment tool. Equally important, improved retention saves money that the company can spend on strategic change initiatives—rather than on hiring and training new employees.

- **Outplacement programs.** During some change initiatives, layoffs are unavoidable. Downsizing can deal a fatal blow to any change effort, so consider ways to lessen the damage and even plant the seeds for successful change later. For example, before managers lay off any employees, ask the managers to think about whether those employees have skills needed in another position or area of the business. Use your own understanding of the skills required across various parts of the business to suggest ways of redeploying valued workers. And ensure that your company provides the most comprehensive outplacement services it can. That way, outgoing employees will be more likely to speak highly of your organization to others in the industry. Again, explain to other executives and managers that this positive word of mouth can cycle back and enable the firm to recruit *and* retain the talent it needs.

Create Results-Driven Change

Too many managers initiate change programs that focus on the activities involved—the minutia of who does what when—at the expense of the desired results. They falsely assume that if the activities are implemented successfully, the desired results will simply materialize. But because there's no explicit connection between actions and outcomes, improvements elude these managers. Instead of focusing only on *activities*, change leaders need to launch *results-driven* improvement programs designed to achieve specific, measurable improvements within a few months.

Results-driven change programs rely on an incremental approach to change—building on what works and discarding what doesn't. Consequently, successes come quickly, and managers build their skills and gain employees' support for future changes.

Robert H. Schaffer and Harvey A. Thomson offer suggestions for getting results-driven change programs up and running:[6]

- **Translate the long-term vision into doable but ambitious short-term goals.** Ask implementation team members to set and achieve a few demanding but immediate performance goals related to the overarching vision behind the change effort—and using the resources at hand. Examples might include faster time to hire, decreased staff turnover, faster responses to customers, lower costs, increased sales, improved cash flow, and so forth. Also ask team members to test process or technical innovations that can help them reach those goals.

- **Periodically review strategy, learning from both successes and failures.** Review and evaluate progress on the array of short-term projects under way. Find out what is and isn't working. See how rapidly project teams can make gains, what kinds of support they need, what process changes they can make quickly, and what obstacles need the attention of upper management. Ditch any practices that aren't generating results. As confidence and momentum grow, refine strategies and timetables and carve out the next round of goals.

- **Institutionalize changes that work—and get rid of the rest.** Embed in the company's way of doing things those practices and technologies that contribute the most to performance improvement. For example, one company discovered that assigning a single manager responsibility for moving each new product from engineering to production and to delivery worked far more smoothly and efficiently than having this responsibility handed off from function to function. The process became standard practice.

Celebrate Milestones

Change initiatives can be long and frustrating. But as you saw in chapter 5, you can keep up peoples' spirits and energy if you identify milestones—even small, short-term wins—and celebrate them as they are achieved. (See "Tips for Celebrating Short-Term Wins.") Celebrating a series of short-term wins can

Tips for Celebrating Short-Term Wins

Here are just a few ideas for celebrating short-term wins and keeping your change team pumped up. You can apply these practices yourself for a change effort you're leading, as well as coach other managers in your firm to use these same practices for initiatives they're leading.

- Treat change participants to a catered lunch—and bring in an outside speaker who can talk about his or her company's success in doing something similar.

- Have a picnic for the change team members.

- Allow the team to take the afternoon off to play or attend a softball game.

- Recognize the deeds of exceptional contributors by writing articles praising them in the company newsletter.

- Give small cash awards or coupons to local theaters or restaurants.

- Provide "scratch cards" that can be redeemed for a variety of small but fun awards.

- Give a handwritten thank-you note to each team member, in which you specify what you appreciate about that person.

- Give each team member a free, one-year subscription to a magazine of his or her choice.

For major successes, do something grander—whatever your company can afford. For example, when your team has successfully reached the initiative's midpoint, consider the following awards.

- Host a dinner for the team, at which the CEO attends as a guest and keynote speaker.

- Give team members an extra week of paid vacation.

- Take the team on a weeklong cruise to an exotic island.

- Pay for team members' gym memberships for a year.

- Reimburse team members' day-care costs for several months or a year.

- Send team members to special seminars, workshops, meetings, or courses outside the company that cover topics of interest to them.

- Coordinate a surprise, catered evening of lavish entertainment for the team—including dinner, dancing, and presentations of awards.

But take care *not* to convey the message that total victory is at hand. Instead, reward what the group *has* achieved—then remind people of the next milestones coming up. So instead of declaring victory, use the credibility and momentum gained from your short-term wins to muster an attack on the next milestone.

- neutralize skepticism about the change effort;

- provide evidence that peoples' sacrifices and hard work are paying off;

- help retain the support of senior management;

- keep up the momentum; and

- boost morale.

Use Consultants Wisely

As an HR professional, you may be called on to hire consultants to help with parts of a major change initiative that you're facilitating.

Or if you're leading a change effort, you may decide yourself to use consultants for part or all of the implementation. Consultants have been working with companies to implement change initiatives since the early post-World War II era, when McKinsey and The Boston Consulting Group began offering strategic planning advice to corporate executives. But the real growth in management consulting came through HR departments when academic work in the social/behavioral sciences—particularly in psychology, sociology, social anthropology, and organizational behavior—found applications (and paying customers) in the world of business. Indeed, many people in the field of management consulting see themselves as conduits through which businesspeople can test and apply concepts developed in the academic realm in the real world.

From those origins, consultants have developed new and more lucrative practices in the field of change management. During the early 1980s, the hottest cards in the deck were total quality management and its offspring: benchmarking, *kaizen* (continuous improvement), and service excellence. A decade later, process reengineering and organizational learning were the favored corporate elixirs. More recently, consulting companies have ridden a wave of interest in enterprise-linking information systems and customer-relationship management systems—and have helped companies design, install, and manage them.

Before enlisting the help of a consultant in your change initiative, it is important to understand how consultants can help you, and how you can make the most of their services. (See appendix B for more information on selecting a consultant.)

With respect to change initiatives, it's useful to think of two types of consultants:

- **Expert consultants** help to shape the context of change. Which strategy needs to change? Which structure? Which systems?

- **Process consultants** recommend ways to make change happen, and help implement those new processes. They also coach the company's leadership and the change team.

Either of these types of consultants augments the organization's official leadership and generally follows this modus operandi:

1. **Diagnosis.** A team of junior consultants gathers information both inside and outside the organization with the goal of: (1) determining where the company stands in terms of some measure of organization performance, and (2) how the company's problems and their root causes relate to that performance measure.

2. **Capabilities assessment.** The team assesses the capabilities of the company's human and physical resources.

3. **Strategy development.** Working with management, the consulting team develops a strategy for reaching the desired level of performance. Depending on the situation, that strategy may include various doses of employee training, process reengineering, organizational restructuring, and new information technology.

4. **Implementation.** Consultant teams provide training and work with employee teams to plan the change program and roll the company's strategy into action.

You'll probably find it most useful to give consultants the lead with some of these steps but use them in advisory roles for others. For example, a consultant is often ideally suited to conduct steps 1 and 2. He or she can be more objective in making a diagnosis and assessing internal capabilities than can an internal team and will likely have intimate knowledge of industry best practices that your own people may lack.

As you move through these steps, consultants should gradually assume background roles. Beginning with the strategy development phase (Step 3), company personnel should start shouldering more and more of the burden, as shown in figure 6-1. After all, it's their program, and they'll have to live with it.

The above steps represent a generalized model, of course. Different types of programs will call for different roles and relation-

FIGURE 6-1

The Roles of Consultants and Employees in Change Programs

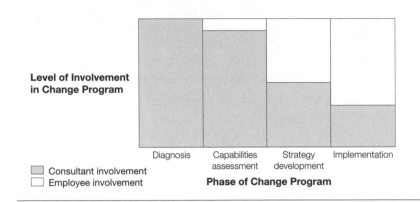

Level of Involvement
in Change Program

Diagnosis   Capabilities   Strategy   Implementation
             assessment   development

☐ Consultant involvement
☐ Employee involvement   **Phase of Change Program**

ships. Consider the Theory E and Theory O approaches described in chapter 2 of this book. As you may recall, Theory E change is a top-down approach that focuses on restructuring the asset base of the business with the goal of producing rapid improvements in shareholder value. Such change relies heavily on consultants, who identify and analyze the problems and shape the solutions. According to authors Michael Beer and Nitin Nohria, "A SWAT team of Ivy League–educated M.B.A.'s, armed with an arsenal of state-of-the-art ideas, is brought in to find new ways to look at the business and manage it. The consultants can help CEOs get a fix on urgent issues and priorities. They also offer much-needed political and psychological support for CEOs who are under fire from financial markets."[7]

Theory O change programs, in contrast, rely far less on consultants. Instead, consultants act as expert resources who prepare and empower employees to do the heavy lifting of change, including business analysis and the crafting of solutions. In effect, this is what happened in General Electric's famous "Work-Out" initiative of the late 1980s—a prototypical Theory O change program. That program aimed to stamp out bureaucracy (which then-CEO Jack Welch loathed) and reshape the operating units to behave more like entrepreneurial small companies. Consultants had the job of organizing New England–style "town meetings" for each of the company's operating units. Small groups of employees were invited to these meetings, where consultants facilitated discussion between bosses and employees on how each group's business could be improved.

Thus, the best approach to using consultants is bound to be heavily situational. If the goal is restructuring, change consultants can and should play a major role—they have very specialized knowledge and experience for these rare events. But if the change involves altering how people work, put your own people in charge and use consultants as facilitators.

Summing Up

This chapter addressed the all-important phase of implementation in a change program. Without effective implementation, all the front-end analysis, strategizing, and planning will be a waste of time and money.

Seven activities were identified as essential for implementation:

- **Enlisting the support and involvement of key people.** This means assembling a team with the right blend of skills, authority, resources, and leadership.

- **Crafting a good implementation plan.** Remember to keep it simple, flexible, divided into achievable chunks, and with clearly defined roles and responsibilities.

- **Communicating relentlessly.** Tell them why, tell them how, and tell them often.

- **Supporting the plan with consistent behaviors.** Make sure that management "walks the talk."

- **Developing "enabling structures."** This means training, pilot programs, and alignment of the rewards system with your change goals.

- **Creating results–driven change.** In other words, link the activities the change effort entails with short-term, measurable, desired outcomes. Build on those small successes to drive further change.

- **Celebrating milestones.** Identify important milestones in the project and celebrate them when they are reached.

Do these well and you'll tilt the odds of success in your favor. The role of consultants was also discussed in this chapter. Exactly how consultants should participate is generally a function of the type of change you're aiming for:

- If the change is restructuring, with the purchase, sale, and/or consolidation of units, consultants will play a large role.

- If the change involves how people work together, company personnel should be prepared to carry the burden of leadership.

Leveraging Chapter Insights: Critical Questions

- Of the seven steps described above, which do change leaders in your company apply most successfully? Which steps do they have the most trouble implementing?

- How might change leaders in your company improve weak areas—whether these areas involve crafting a change-implementation plan, developing enabling structures, celebrating milestones, or some other aspect of putting a change initiative into motion?

- Think of a major change effort you're leading or facilitating. Based on the nature of the initiative, how might you make the *best* use of consultants to implement the initiative?

CHAPTER SEVEN

How Employees Respond to Change

A Continuum of Styles

Key Topics Covered in This Chapter

- *Common responses to change*

- *Change resisters, and how to deal with them*

- *Change agents—the people who can make things happen*

ORGANIZATIONS are inherently social systems. The people operating within these systems have identities, relationships, communities, attitudes, and emotions. They also have different degrees of power and influence, as well as different ways through which they exercise those powers. So when you try to change any part of the system, all of these factors come into play, adding complexity to a change process. Successful management of change requires that you recognize the primacy of people factors and the social systems in which human beings operate.

People respond to change in a wide variety of ways. Each way has unique characteristics, and each requires a different style of management.

Common Responses to Change

People also develop routines. Think about your own routine on a typical weekend morning. Sleep until 8:00. Start a load of laundry. Cook the nice breakfast you never have time to make during the week. Pay the week's bills. Take the dog for a walk to the park. Chances are that you have routines at work as well. Like the woodland deer, people follow trails that are familiar, comfortable, safe, and satisfying. And they aren't eager to change unless given compelling reasons to do so. People also have "social routines" at work—associations with coworkers that satisfy their needs as social animals. Changes that impinge on those routines are equally unwelcome.

Occasional diversions from routines and existing social patterns add variety and interest—which please us. But diversions may also create tension, anxiety, discomfort, and even fear. As the late longshoreman-philosopher Eric Hoffer wrote in *The Ordeal of Change*: "It is my impression that no one really likes the new. We are afraid of it." He notes that even small changes from the routine can be upsetting.

> *Back in 1936 I spent a good part of the year picking peas. I started out early in January in the Imperial Valley [of California] and drifted northward, picking peas as they ripened, until I picked the last peas of the season in June, around Tracy. Then I shifted all the way to Lake County, where for the first time I was going to pick string beans. And I still remember how hesitant I was that first morning as I was about to address myself to the string bean vines. Would I be able to pick string beans? Even the change from peas to string beans had in it elements of fear.*
>
> *In the case of drastic change the uneasiness is of course deeper and more lasting. We can never be really prepared for that which is wholly new. We have to adjust ourselves and every radical adjustment is a crisis in self-esteem: we undergo a test, we have to prove ourselves. It needs inordinate self-confidence to face drastic change without inner trembling.*[1]

Certainly no two people feel the same "trembling" described by Hoffer. And some individuals are absolutely energized by change. The Myers-Briggs personality framework addresses this broad spectrum. At one end of the spectrum, for example, it describes a person who likes a planned and organized approach to life (a "judging" person). He or she likes things settled. At the other end of the spectrum is the "perceiving" person who prefers open options and a flexible and spontaneous approach to life.[2] You probably have people representing both types in your organization, and as an HR manager who will be leading or facilitating change, you need to learn to deal with the full range of personalities. In particular:

- Think about the people who will participate in your change initiative. Who will react negatively to having their routines disrupted, and who will positively enjoy the experience? Make a list.

- Once you've identified people likely to be uncomfortable with change, think about their roles in the change initiative. They probably aren't the ones you'll want in key positions where initiative and enthusiasm are needed. Think, too, about how these individuals can be helped through the process.

- For individuals with pro-change dispositions, consider ways to optimize the energy they bring to the program, and how they can work with others.

And don't forget about yourself. Like everyone else, you have a unique disposition to change. You either love it, hate it, or (more likely) you're somewhere between those extremes.

Discovery Learning, Inc. of Greensboro, North Carolina, has developed a helpful methodology for measuring an individual's disposition to change, indicating where that person is likely to fall on a "preferred style" continuum.[3] In their model, "Conservers" occupy one end of the continuum. Conservers are people who prefer current circumstances over the unknown—people who are more comfortable with gradual change than with anything radical. Occupying the opposite end of the spectrum are the "Originators," who prefer more rapid and radical change. "Originators are representative of the reengineering approach to change," according to Discovery Learning. "The goal of an Originator is to challenge existing structure, resulting in fast, fundamentally different, even systemic changes."[4] Occupying a middle position between these two extremes are the "Pragmatists" who support change when it clearly addresses current challenges. Pragmatists are less wedded to the existing structure than to structures that are likely to be suc-

TABLE 7-1

A Continuum of Change-Response Styles

Change-Response Style	Common Behaviors
"Conservers"	• Appear deliberate, disciplined, and organized • Prefer change that maintains current structure • Operate from conventional assumptions • Enjoy predictability • Appear cautious and inflexible • Focus on details and routine • Honor tradition and established practice
"Pragmatists"	• Appear practical, agreeable, flexible • Prefer change emphasizing workable outcomes • Focused on results more than structure • Operate as mediators and catalysts for understanding • Are open to both sides of an argument • Take a middle-of-the-road approach • Are team-oriented
"Originators"	• Appear unorganized, undisciplined, unconventional, and spontaneous • Prefer change that challenges current structure • Challenge accepted assumptions • Enjoy risk and uncertainty • May be impractical and miss important details • May appear visionary and systemic in their thinking • Can treat accepted policies and procedures with little regard

Source: W. Christopher Musselwhite and Robyn Ingram, *Change Style Indicator* (Greensboro, NC: The Discovery Learning Press, 1999), 5–7. Used with permission.

cessful. (See table 7-1 for more on how Discovery Learning generalizes the characteristics of people who represent these three change style preferences.)

Knowing where your coworkers stand—and where you stand—in a change preference continuum such as this one can help you more effectively manage the people side of a change initiative.

The Resisters

"The reformer has enemies in all those who profit by the old order," Machiavelli warned his readers. And what held true in six-teenth-century Italy remains true today. Some people clearly enjoy advantages that—rightly or wrongly—they view as threatened by change. They may perceive change as endangering their liveli-hoods, their perks, their workplace social arrangements, or their status in the organization. Others know that their specialized skills will be rendered less valuable after a major change. For example, when a supplier of automotive hydraulic steering systems switched in the late 1990s to electronic steering technology, employees with expertise in hoses, valves, and fluid pressure were suddenly less important. The know-how they had developed over long careers now had less value for the company.

Paul Strebel provides another explanation of what causes resist-ance to change.[5] In his view:

> Top-level managers see change as an opportunity to strengthen the business by aligning operations with strategy, to take on new profes-sional challenges and risks, and to advance their careers. For many employees, however, including middle managers, change is neither sought after nor welcomed. It is disruptive and intrusive. It upsets the balance.

Strebel believes that resistance occurs because change alters the terms of *personal compacts* between employees and organizations— reciprocal obligations and mutual commitments, stated and implied, that define their relationship. Unless change leaders define *new* terms and persuade employees to accept them, they can't realisti-cally expect employees to support changes that alter the status quo.

Strebel identifies three major dimensions shared by all personal compacts, as shown in table 7-2.

Any time people perceive themselves as losers in a change ini-tiative, or fail to understand how change affects their personal compacts with the company, you can expect resistance. Resistance may be passive, in the form of noncommitment to the goals and the

TABLE 7-2

Dimensions of Personal Compacts

Dimension	Definition	Questions Employees Ask
Formal	Tasks and performance requirements for a job, as defined by job descriptions, employment contracts, and performance agreements	• "What am I supposed to do for the organization?" • "What help will I get to do the job?" • "How and when will my performance be evaluated, and what form will the feedback take?" • "What will I be paid, and how will pay relate to my performance evaluation?"
Psychological	An employee's personal commitment to individual and company objectives	• "How hard will I really have to work?" • "What recognition, financial reward, or other personal satisfaction will I get for my efforts?" • "Are the rewards worth it?"
Social	Employees' perceptions of the company's mission, values, and integrity	• "Are my values similar to those of others in the organization?" • "What are the real rules that determine who gets what in this company?"

Source: Paul Strebel, "Why Do Employees Resist Change?" in *Harvard Business Review on Change* (Boston: Harvard Business School Press), 142–145.

process for reaching them. Or it may be active, in the form of direct opposition or subversion. How will you deal with that resistance?

Change masters have dealt with resisters in different ways over the years. French revolutionaries used the guillotine. The Bolsheviks had resisters shot or packed off to the gulags. Mao and his communist followers sent them to "reeducation" camps. Thankfully, employment laws have barred such techniques from the corporate change master's tool kit. And there *are* other things you can do to address resistance—and to help other executives and managers do the same. Begin by identifying potential resisters and working to redirect them in support of change. Here are some guidelines you can follow as well as offer other managers who must address resistance:

- Ask yourself, "Where and how will change create pain or loss in my organization?"

- Identify people who have something to lose, and anticipate how they will respond.

- Communicate the "why" of change to potential resisters. Explain the urgency of moving away from established routines or arrangements.

- Emphasize the benefits of change to potential resisters— for example, greater future job security, higher pay, and so forth. There's no guarantee that the benefits of change will exceed the losses for these individuals. However, explaining the benefits will help shift their focus from negatives to positives.

- Help resisters find new roles—roles that represent genuine contributions *and* mitigate their losses.

- Remember that many people resist change because it represents a loss of control over their daily lives. Return some of that control by making resisters active partners in the change program.

If these interventions fail, move resisters out of your unit. You cannot afford to let a few disgruntled individuals subvert the progress of the entire group. But don't make them "walk the plank." Do what you can to relocate them to positions where their particular skills can be better used. That's what the innovator of electronic steering systems did. That company still had plenty of business supplying hydraulic systems to car and truck manufacturers, so it employed its hydraulic specialists in those units even as it hired electronic engineers for its expanding new business.

As you consider resisters, don't forget that your own approach to initiating or managing change may be contributing to the problem. "Technical" solutions imposed from the outside often breed resistance because they fail to recognize the social dimension of work. Paul Lawrence made this point many years ago in his classic *Harvard Business Review* article "How to Deal with Resistance to Change."[6] In looking at interrelationships among employees, Lawrence found that change originating among employees who work closely together is usually implemented smoothly. But change imposed by outsiders threatens powerful social bonds, generating resentment and resistance. So be sure to evaluate what part you may be playing in the resistance problem.

Dealing with Passive Resisters

Earlier, we described passive resistance to change as noncommitment to goals and the process for reaching them. Passive resisters frustrate managers. While they don't sabotage the program, they certainly don't help the initiative move forward.

The reason that a person won't change, explain psychologists Robert Kegan and Lisa Laskow Lahey, is that he or she has a "competing commitment"—a subconscious, hidden goal that conflicts with the *stated* commitment.[7] For example, a project leader who is dragging his feet may have an unrecognized competing commitment to avoid tougher assignments that may come his way if he's too successful with the current project. A supervisor who cannot seem to get on board with the new team-based approach to problem-solving may be worried that she will be seen as incompetent if she cannot solve problems herself.

Though competing commitments are likely to be lodged deep in an employee's psyche, some serious probing on your part can sometimes get them to the surface, where you and the employee can deal with them. The most practical advice here is to engage in one-on-one communication with the passive resister. You need to find out what's keeping this person from participating in an active way.

The Change Agents

Think for a moment about the big, big changes in the world over the centuries. Chances are that you can associate individuals with each of those changes. Copernicus and Galileo ultimately changed our view of where we stand relative to our neighbors in the solar system. Martin Luther split Christendom in two and contributed indirectly to the rise of nation states in Europe. Charles Darwin's theory on natural selection torpedoed the accepted wisdom on humankind's history. Karl Marx, a thinker, and Vladimir Lenin, a doer, created a communist movement that, at its apex, held sway over almost half the world. Henry Ford and his engineers developed a new approach to manufacturing—the assembly line—that fundamentally altered the auto and many other industries. In each of these cases, someone who thought differently had a major impact on human history. None began with serious resources or backing, all were outsiders, and all faced substantial opposition. All were what we call *change agents*.

Many change agents operate outside of the existing power structure. They are catalysts who get the ball rolling, even if they do not necessarily do most of the pushing. Everett Rogers described them as figures with one foot in the old world and one in the new—creators of a bridge across which others can travel.[8] They help others to see what the problems are, and convince them to grapple with them. Change agents, in Rogers' view, fulfill critical roles. They

- articulate the need for change;

- are accepted by others as trustworthy and competent (people must accept the messenger before they accept the message);

- see and diagnose problems from the perspective of their audience;

- motivate people to change;

- work through others in translating intent into action;

- stabilize the adoption of innovation; and

- foster self-renewing behavior in others so that they can "go out of business" as change agents.

Who in your organization has these characteristics? Are you one of them? It is important to identify the change agents so that you can place them in key positions during a change effort. In a self-regenerating company, you'll find change agents in many different operating units and at all different levels. (See "Tips for Identifying Change Agents" for more information.)

Can change agents be created? Perhaps. One German electronics firm did so in the 1990s when it faced poor financial performance, sagging morale, and weak competitiveness. The company was over-consulted and under-managed. Many of its best young employees were unhappy with consecutive years of losses and dimming

Tips for Identifying Change Agents

- Find out who people listen to. Change agents lead with the power of their ideas. But be warned: These may not be employees with formal authority to lead.

- Be alert to people who "think otherwise." Change agents are not satisfied with things as they are—a fact that may not endear them to management.

- Take a close look at new employees who have come from outside the circle of traditional competitors. They may not be infected with the same mind-set as everyone else.

- Look for people with unusual training or experience. For example, if all your marketing people have business degrees and heavy quantitative research backgrounds, look for the oddball liberal arts major who has a degree in social anthropology. Chances are he sees the world through a different lens.

prospects. The company's rigid corporate hierarchy was partly to blame. Management recognized that it had to distribute authority and decision making more broadly. To accomplish this it created a change-agent program that sent two dozen hand-picked employees to the United States for special training, which included abundant exposure to entrepreneurial American firms. Once the training program was completed, the newly minted change agents were transferred back to their units, where they worked to break the mold of the old hierarchical system.

General Motors attempted something very similar in its joint venture with Toyota: the NUMMI small car assembly plant in California. That plant was run according to Toyota's world-beating production methods, and GM rotated manufacturing managers through the plant to learn Toyota's methods and, hopefully, bring a working knowledge of those methods back to Detroit. Furniture maker Herman Miller sought the same result when it moved managers from its SQA unit into its traditional operating units; it figured that these individuals would infect others with their faster, more accurate approach to manufacturing and fulfillment.

Your search for change agents shouldn't necessarily be limited to company personnel. Every so often it's wise to look outside for people who have the skills and attitudes required to stir things up and get the organization moving in a new and more promising direction. This approach is not without risk, since the outsiders' lack of familiarity with the company's culture may result in unforeseen turmoil. For a discussion of this issue, see "The Insider-Outsider as Change Agent" and its *Harvard Business Review* excerpt.

Summing Up

Change is complicated by the fact that organizations are social systems whose participants have identities, relationships, communities, routines, emotions, and differentiated powers. Thus managers must be alert to how a change will conflict with existing social systems and individual routines.

The Insider-Outsider as Change Agent

Many companies feel that the only way to create change and make it stick is to bring in outsiders with no ties to the status quo. Others fear that outsiders who don't understand the business, its culture, and its values will simply create disruption. Writing in the *Harvard Business Review*, Donald Sull recommends that leadership for change be invested in individuals who represent both sides of the coin—a fresh perspective on the business *and* a solid appreciation for the company's culture:

> *Guiding a company through big changes requires a difficult balancing act. The company's heritage has to be respected even as it's being resisted. It's often assumed that outsider managers are best suited to lead such an effort since they're not bound by the company's historical formula. . . . Typically, outsiders are so quick to throw out all the old ways of working that they end up doing more harm than good.*
>
> *The approach I recommend is to look for new leaders from within the company but from outside the core business. These managers, whom I call insider-outsiders, can be drawn from the company's smaller divisions, from international operations, or from staff functions. . . .*
>
> *Insider-outsiders have led many of the most dramatic corporate transformations in recent times. Jack Welch spent most of his career in GE's plastics business; Jürgen Schrempp was posted in South Africa before returning to run [DaimlerChrysler]; and Domenico De Sole served as the Gucci Group's legal counsel before leading that company's dramatic rejuvenation.*
>
> *Another alternative is to assemble management teams that leverage the strengths of both insiders and outsiders. When [Lou] Gerstner took over at IBM, he didn't force out all the old guard. Most operating positions continued to be staffed by IBM veterans with decades of experience, but they were supported by outsiders*

Continued

> *in key staff slots and marketing roles. The combination of per-*
> *spectives has allowed IBM to use old strengths to fuel its passage*
> *down an entirely new course.*
>
> *Finally, inside managers can break free of their old formulas*
> *by imagining themselves as outsiders, as Intel's executives did in*
> *deciding to abandon the memory business. Intel had pioneered the*
> *market for memory chips, and for most of its executives, employ-*
> *ees, and customers, Intel meant memory. As new competitors*
> *entered the market, however, Intel saw its share of the memory*
> *business dwindle. . . . Although Intel had built an attractive*
> *microprocessor business during this time, it clung to the memory*
> *business until its chairman, Gordon Moore, and its president,*
> *Andy Grove, sat down and deliberately imagined what would*
> *happen if they were replaced with outsiders. They agreed that*
> *outsiders would get out of the memory business—and that's*
> *exactly what Moore and Grove did. While a company's competi-*
> *tive formula exerts a tremendous gravitational pull, thinking like*
> *outsiders can help insiders to break free.*

SOURCE: Donald N. Sull, "Why Good Companies Go Bad," *Harvard Business Review* (July–August 1999): 50.

This chapter explored common responses to change and ways to deal with resisters and identify change agents:

- **Common responses to change** can be seen as existing along a continuum. This chapter adopted the terms "conservers," "pragmatists," and "originators" to describe how different people respond to change. Knowing where your coworkers stand—and where you stand—in a change preference continuum such as this one can help you be more effective in managing the people side of a change initiative.

- **Change resisters** will either drag their feet or actively attempt to undermine your efforts. You can identify potential resisters by determining where and how change will create pain or loss in the organization. Once you've identified them, there are several things you can do to neutralize their resistance or make them active participants. The actions include: explaining the urgent need to change, describing how change will produce benefits for them, and finding new ways in which they can contribute. People who do not respond to these efforts should be moved out of your unit.

- **Change agents** see the need for change and articulate it effectively to others. They are critical catalysts for a change initiative and should be placed in key positions. This chapter has provided tips for identifying change agents.

Leveraging Chapter Insights: Critical Questions

- Where do *you* fit on the continuum of common responses to change?

- Where are the "conservers," "pragmatists," and "originators" in your organization?

- Think of a change initiative you're about to lead or facilitate. What kinds of losses would the initiative impose on employees? What alterations to personal compacts will be necessary owing to the change? How might you persuade employees to accept those new terms?

- Who might be active and passive resistors in your company? Who might be change agents?

CHAPTER EIGHT

Helping Employees Adapt to Change

Strategies to Reduce Stress

Key Topics Covered in This Chapter

- *The four stages of reaction to change: shock, defensive retreat, acknowledgment, and acceptance and adaptation*

- *How individuals can help themselves navigate change*

- *How HR managers can help employees and themselves cope with change*

- *Alternative ways for HR managers to think about change resisters*

THE BUSINESS PRESS and many academics like to talk about the importance of change, and how it makes us all better people and more satisfied with and fulfilled by our work. They extol the virtues of "thriving" on chaos and encourage us to "embrace" change as if it were something we just can't get enough of. In reality, change puts lots of people through the wringer—particularly Theory E change, which aims to quickly increase shareholder value. Far from "thriving," some employees don't survive the change program at all, let alone come out in one piece. Both unsuccessful and successful change programs produce stress, and many result in the displacement of good people. Ask the thousands of General Electric employees who lost their jobs when Jack Welch pared down his company to a manageable set of future-facing businesses. These hapless men and women didn't call the CEO Neutron Jack for nothing. The same goes for "Chain-saw" Al Dunlap, who lopped off great chunks of the employment ranks at Scott Paper in a major corporate makeover. Ask the people who survived several rounds of downsizing at IBM and Cisco Systems about "embracing" change.

In these types of changes, survivors are almost universally left shell-shocked. Morale shrivels, trust in the company hits rock bottom, and employee loyalty evaporates. As an HR professional, you can't restore the old, familiar, safe world for change survivors, but you *can* help them through the turmoil, and get them back into a productive frame of mind. This chapter describes the stress caused by workplace change and provides guidelines for how you can help people through it.

Loss and Anxiety

The typical employee spends at least eight hours a day doing fairly routine tasks. Indeed, when companies talk about their "culture," they imply a certain measure of stability and routine. They reinforce that stability with job descriptions that prescribe in concrete terms what employees should do day-to-day and week-to-week. There's a tangible agreement that if an employee does X, and does it well and on time, he or she will receive Y in compensation and be viewed as a company member in good standing.

There is also a psychological contract between employee and company: As long as the employee fits into work and social patterns, he or she "belongs." And there is a political dimension as well, which demands that career-minded employees play according to certain written and unwritten "rules of the game." But what happens when the contract or rules are changed unexpectedly? Consider this example:

> *This morning we got a memo addressed to "all staff." It said that year-end performance bonuses are being discontinued. Just like that—20 percent of my salary out the window! And after all the long hours I've put in during the last months. . . .*

How do you suppose this person felt? She definitely experienced a loss. Losses caused by change programs usually aren't as drastic as this, however. They are more likely to be a change in job description, or a perceived loss in turf, status, or professional identity. They tend to be threats to values that someone has built up, rather than monetary losses.

Even a positive change can create anxiety for some people. For example, a person who's given a promotion may wonder: Can I handle the job? How will my friendships with people in the department be affected now that I'm their boss? Will the required travel and longer hours create problems at home?

Those questions reflect a fear of the unknown, which often accompanies a loss of certainty. For most people, however, the negative aspects of change are related to a loss of control—over their incomes and influence, their sources of pride, and their familiar ways of living and working. When these factors are threatened, expect to see anxiety and anger.

Reacting to Change: Four Stages

Most people eventually adapt and reconcile themselves to change, but not before passing through various psychological stages. One way to think about those stages is through the concept of risk. According to one theory, change requires people to perform or perceive in unfamiliar ways, which involves risks. Those risks can threaten a person's self-esteem.[1] Understandably, people feel uncomfortable with risk and tend to avoid it when they can. When they cannot, however—as when they're roped into a corporate change initiative—adaptation to change tends to proceed through predictable psychological stages. In some respects, these stages resemble the grieving process a person experiences after the loss of a loved one. The four stages are:[2]

1. **Shock.** In the shock phase, people feel threatened by anticipated change. They may even deny its existence: "This isn't happening." They become immobilized and often shut down in order to protect themselves. People feel unsafe, timid, and unable to act, much less take risks. Needless to say, productivity drops during this stage.

2. **Defensive retreat.** People caught in a change vortex move from shock to defensive retreat. They get angry and lash out at what has been done to them, even as they cling to accustomed ways of doing things. They attempt to keep a grip on the past while decrying the fact that life has changed. This

conflict likewise precludes taking risks; people perceive the situation as too unsafe for risk-taking.

3. **Acknowledgment.** Eventually, most people cease denying the fact of change, and acknowledge that they have lost something. They mourn. The psychological dynamics of this stage include both grief and liberation. Thus, one can feel like a pawn in a game while also being able to view that game with some degree of objectivity and psychological distance. During this stage, the notion of taking risks becomes more palatable, and people begin to explore the pros and cons of the new situation. Each "risk" that proves successful builds confidence and prepares people for more.

4. **Acceptance and adaptation.** Most people ultimately internalize the change, make any needed adaptations, and move on. They see themselves "before and after" the change. Even if it's a grudging acknowledgment, they consider the change "for the best." In some cases, people actively advocate for what they had previously opposed. Acceptance and adaptation means relinquishing the old situation—as well as the pain, confusion, and fear experienced in the earlier stages of change.

Progress through these four stages is linear, and you and other managers should accelerate the process only with great care. Speeding up the process risks forcing people to carry unfinished psychological "baggage" from one phase to the next. Thus, you may need to resist any natural bias toward fast action, and exercise patience instead. Encourage other managers to do the same. The expression "time heals all wounds" says it well enough.

This theory about how people deal with and eventually accept change is somewhat simplistic. Although most people work through the four emotional stages—some more quickly than others—some will get stuck in defensive retreat and channel their energies into resistance.

People get stuck for two basic and obvious reasons: First, change is not a single event with neat and tidy beginnings and endings;

and second, people's experiences with change vary with individual circumstance. Thus, frameworks like the one described above are far from perfect. To further complicate matters, change often hits from two or more directions at the same time. For example, a division of a large corporation is put through a wrenching restructuring in which many people are laid off; the same division is then sold to another corporation, which results in new leadership and new policies. Coming all at once (or in rapid sequence), these multiple changes can severely stress or undo the anchor points of those employees and managers who remain. Agreed-upon ways of working, affiliations, skills, and professional identities are all upended—immobilizing people or throwing them into a self-defense mode. In a worst-case scenario, the individual under siege at the office is simultaneously experiencing major change at home—a divorce, for example.

People who are emotionally fragile are at the greatest risk during change initiatives. They typically have the greatest difficulty handling feelings of loss and may choose to see themselves as victims of the process. A perception of victimhood will always hinder an employee's ability to move on after change has occurred.

The Conventional Advice

Some managers attempt to accelerate adaptation to change, and for understandable reasons: Employees who are preoccupied with their internal issues are not fully productive. Indeed, people in the early stages of change are often unable to do much at all. It thus makes good business sense for managers to help them cope and move forward. Unfortunately, such good intentions are often viewed as manipulative, controlling, or autocratic. If the benefits of change are overly hyped, if there are too many pep rallies and too many "it's really good for you" assurances, people grow cynical and dig in their heels: "How can they say everything is rosy when I feel as though I've been stabbed in the back?"

So, what can you do to minimize the negative aspects of change for people in your organization? If you notice some managers in your company who may be trying to push employees hard to adapt to change too quickly, encourage them to share the following guidelines with their employees:

- Keep your cool in dealing with others.

- Do your best to handle pressure smoothly and effectively.

- Respond nondefensively when others disagree with you.

- Develop creative and innovative solutions to problems.

- Be willing to take risks and try out new ideas.

- Be willing to adjust priorities to changing conditions.

- Demonstrate enthusiasm for and commitment to long-term goals.

- Be open and candid when dealing with others.

- Participate actively in the change process.

- Make clear-cut decisions as needed.

This is all good advice, but it fails to take into account psychological needs that must be addressed. Most people are aware of the wisdom of taking responsibility for dealing with change themselves; they recognize the importance of the "right attitude," and they're capable of helping themselves through a difficult change using various strategies. However, people *don't* want this "take the right attitude" message shoved down their throats. Rather, they want some empathy and some understanding of what they are experiencing. They are less interested in advice than in understanding and support.

The next two sections explore ways in which people facing change can help themselves. The sections also provide guidelines that you can use to help managers (and yourself) aid employees in coping with difficult parts of the change process.

What Individuals Can Do for Themselves

The strong emotions that most of us feel at the onset of change—anger, depression, and shock—are not useful. They neither comfort us nor move us forward. But they must be acknowledged and addressed. We have rational *and* emotional sides of our beings, and each must be paid its due. (See "Tips for Recognizing the Emotional Side.") The secret to success? Provide the following guidelines to managers for helping their employees to express the emotional side while gradually passing control to the rational side.

Overcome Powerlessness

A feeling of powerlessness, or loss of control, is a major cause of change-related distress among employees. Someone over whom

---

Tips for Recognizing the Emotional Side

- Remind managers that their employees' anger, depression, and shock are natural reactions to loss. People need to give themselves permission to feel what they are feeling. Change always involves a loss of some kind: a job, colleagues, a role, even one's professional identity. That loss must be duly acknowledged and mourned.

- Encourage managers to let direct reports' mourning take its course.

- Urge managers to be patient and to recognize that people need time to come to grips with a situation and move through the various stages. Employees can't do it overnight, and no single time line works for everyone. But warn managers against letting people wallow in self-pity and grief—this kind of behavior is ultimately unproductive and can even damage team morale.

they have no control has arbitrarily upset their routines of work, sold off the division, laid off many of their workplace friends, or altered the compensation system. Worse, employees have no recourse.

One antidote to feeling powerless is for employees to establish a sense of personal control in other areas of their lives. For example, someone might take charge of his or her investment club's monthly newsletter. Someone else might design a room addition to his or her home. These actions all represent ways to regain a sense of personal control and vanquish feelings of powerlessness. Another antidote is to avoid taking on other efforts that sap energy. Thus, if adapting to change is arduous, individuals should marshal their resources. (See "Tips for Marshaling Resources.")

Inventory a Change Initiative's Gains and Losses

Accepting strong emotions and acknowledging the importance of patience in dealing with change are vital managerial activities— but so is developing objectivity about what is happening. People have choices in how they perceive change, and they can develop the capacity to see benefits, not just losses, in new situations. Coming to accept and adapt to change is in fact a process of balancing what's been lost with what's being gained. This is far different from merely "looking on the bright side." Inventorying personal losses and gains is a tangible step that people can take in gathering the strength to move on. See assessment tool 8-1 for a worksheet that helps you inventory the gains and losses—for yourself, employees, and managers—associated with a change initiative at your company. You might also give this worksheet to managers in your company and suggest that they customize it to help themselves and their employees assess gains and losses that will come with a major change.

Re-anchor

"Re-anchoring" is related to inventorying gains and losses. Here, the individual balances the emotional investment in essential

Tips for Marshaling Resources

To regain a sense of personal control, people need to maintain their physical well-being as well as nourish their psyches. Encourage managers throughout your firm to advocate the following simple but powerful practices for themselves and their employees:

- Get enough sleep.

- Eat right and get regular exercise.

- Take occasional breaks at the office.

- Relax with friends.

- Engage in hobbies.

- Talk about the situation with supportive friends, a mental-health professional, or clergy member.

- Indulge in something particularly enjoyable—a movie, a visit to a spa, a trip to a favorite museum.

- Practice meditation, deep breathing, or other relaxation disciplines, such as tai chi, qi gong, or yoga.

- Devote a specific amount of time each morning—say, 10 minutes—to worrying in a concentrated way about the upcoming day.

These are not forms of escapism, nor do they distract a person from reality. Rather, they are practical ways by which an employee can exert control over his or her life during a period of flux.

work-related "anchors"—daily work routines, affiliations, skills, professional identity—with emotional investments in other areas, such as family, friends, and civic and religious activities. Thus, when one or more workplace anchors is set adrift, the person can remain steady by creating or strengthening anchors elsewhere. See

Assessment Tool 8-1
Take Stock of a Change Initiative's Losses and Gains

Think of a major change initiative that is occurring at your company. Use this mini-worksheet to assess the losses and gains associated with the initiative.

Type of change that is occurring:

Losses/Gains for Myself

My possible losses owing to the change:

-
-
-

My possible gains owing to the change:

-
-
-

Ways I can cope with or adapt to these losses:

-
-
-

Ways I can maximize these gains:

-
-
-

Losses/Gains for Employees

Employees' possible losses owing to the change:

-
-
-

Continued

Employees' possible gains owing to the change:
-
-
-

Ways I can help employees maximize these gains:
-
-
-

Ways I can help employees cope with or adapt to these losses:
-
-
-

Losses/Gains for Managers

Managers' possible losses owing to the change:
-
-
-

Managers' possible gains owing to the change:
-
-
-

Ways I can help managers cope with or adapt to these losses:
-
-
-

Ways I can help managers maximize these gains:
-
-
-

"Tips for Re-Anchoring" for more on this. Also consider giving this list to managers throughout your firm, to help them aid themselves and their direct reports in re-anchoring.

Admittedly, inventorying and re-anchoring are difficult when a person is in the grip of strong emotions. Perhaps the best mecha-

Tips for Re-Anchoring

Suppose a workplace change has resulted in an employee's transfer to a new department in which he or she has no real friends. In this case, the person could re-anchor by applying the following strategies

Developing new friendships in the department:
- Inviting people to lunch. At lunch, ask people about their interests—looking in particular for shared hobbies or activities.
- Offering assistance to the new colleagues during the workday.
- Joining the department softball team, crafts group, or other social gatherings the department offers.
- Suggesting new ideas for fun departmental activities— such as a movie-discussion group that meets once a month during lunch, or a "Department Night at the Game," whereby your department attends a local baseball or football game.

Solidifying friendships outside work:
- Attending a book club meeting the person has skipped for the past year.
- Having dinner once a week with various friends he or she hasn't seen in a while.
- Committing to phoning long-distance friends who haven't been in touch in ages.
- Planning a weekend excursion with friends.

nism for coping with change, then, is anticipating it. No one escapes the effects of change—in the workplace or elsewhere. However, those who recognize that its impact will be powerful, that the process of adaptation and acceptance takes time, and that we all have multiple sources of strength, are much better positioned to survive change than those who get caught flat-footed.

Helping Managers Assist Their Employees During Change

Many managers find that addressing straightforward, technical issues in the change effort—such as the new department layout, or who gets what training—is comparatively easy. But consciously or not, they ignore the more complex and unpredictable concerns of people being changed. The rationale may be a business one: "We don't have time for that; we're here to make money." Or it may be emotional: "I don't want to get involved in messy feelings; that's not my job."

Ignoring the human side of change, however, is shortsighted and a symptom of ineffective management. Managers are paid to get things done with the human and financial resources given to them—imperfect as those resources may be. Like infantry platoon leaders in a skirmish, they must muster all the firepower at their disposal—and that means getting every one of their people engaged. They cannot afford to write off people who are too afraid to move. They have to get everyone into the fight. And that sometimes means helping direct reports through their fear.

As an HR professional, you can—and must—play an active role in helping managers throughout your firm to guide themselves and their employees through each of the four stages described earlier. Below we take a closer look at what you can do to fulfill this role. (And as always, you can apply these same practices to managing your own employees during a difficult change effort.)

Stage One: Shock

Remind managers throughout your organization that effective leaders prepare people for change long before the shock hits. Military organizations, for instance, don't wait until the heat of battle to deal with the shock it induces in people. Instead, they prepare soldiers for what lies ahead through rigorous training and simulations. Likewise, managers throughout your organization can prepare their people for the shock of change by periodically inoculating them with small doses of it. Offer these guidelines to help your managers with this stage of change—and apply them yourself when you're leading a change within your own department:

- Alter work processes whenever you see real opportunities for improvement.

- Give people periodic reassignments that force them to learn new things and deal with new situations.

- Use stretch goals to encourage flexibility and greater effort.

- Never allow anyone to get too comfortable in his or her job.

- Root out any sense of entitlement.

If you help managers prepare their people for change, they will experience less shock when a really big shake-up hits their unit. Preparation is probably the most important thing you can advocate as a change leader. Even with good preparation, however, there's bound to be shock, and managers will have to deal with the denial, "shutting down," and timidity that characterize this stage. In this case, explain how managers can apply some "first aid":

- If people have had the anchors of their work lives yanked away, find new ones for them to latch onto; for example, their new roles in their new work groups.

- Provide opportunities for people to vent their feelings.

- Be a good listener, but avoid trying to sell employees on the idea that things are actually better for them—they are not yet ready to hear this.

- Help employees manage the stress that results from change (see the "Manage Stress" checklist in appendix A).

Stage Two: Defensive Retreat

People in the stage of defensive retreat get angry and lash out even as they try to hold on to the old ways of doing things. This behavior reduces their productivity. Here are a couple strategies you can offer managers to help them guide their employees through this stage:

- **Keep "retreaters" connected to the immediate group.** An employee's immediate work group is the strongest anchor there is. Individuals who find themselves decoupled from their familiar social arrangements are likely to suffer the most damage, since the group acts as a source of identity, safety, and support. The military, which has enormous experience in this area, emphasizes what it calls "small group cohesion." It knows that soldiers will do remarkable things as members of small, closely knit groups (see "The Power of Small Group Cohesion"). You should do the same by helping people connect to others in their new circumstances. Group activities, lunchtime meetings, or outings all help build connections between strangers.

- **Provide an outlet for people to voice the grievances and angst that need to be vented.** When management provides opportunities for grievances and frustrations to be aired constructively, employees' bitterness and frustration may diminish.

Stage Three: Acknowledgment

Eventually, most people stop denying the fact of change and acknowledge their new situation. The psychological dynamics of this stage include both grief for what has been lost and nascent feelings of liberation. Though they continue to feel like pawns in a game controlled by others, they begin to view that game with a certain amount of distance and objectivity. Risk-taking becomes possible as people begin to explore the pros and cons of the new situation.

You can help managers guide themselves and their employees through this stage by coaching them on these techniques:

- **Be a sounding board.** Continue your role as a sounding board for employees' complaints and questions. Ask, "How do you feel about this?" to get a fix on an individual's emotional state. But begin now to stress the benefits of the new situation.

The Power of Small Group Cohesion

Biographer/historian William Manchester was wounded during the bloody World War II battle to take the Japanese-held
island of Okinawa. Although Manchester had a "ticket home"
wound, he skipped out of the field hospital and rejoined his
unit of U.S. Marines, who were still in the thick of combat.
Many years later he recollected the motivation that propelled
him to put his life on the line (again). His account underscores
the power of small group cohesion—something that every
change manager must appreciate:

*And then, in one of those great thundering jolts in which a man's
real motives are revealed to him in an electrifying vision, I understand, at last, why I jumped hospital that Sunday thirty-five years
ago, and, in violation of orders, returned to the front and almost certain death. It was an act of love. Those men on the line were my
family, my home. . . . They had never let me down, and I couldn't
do it to them. I had to be with them rather than to let them die
and me live with the knowledge that I might have saved them.
Men, I now knew, do not fight for flag or country, for the Marine
Corps or glory or any other abstraction. They fight for one another.*

SOURCE: William Manchester, *Goodbye Darkness* (Boston: Little, Brown and Company, 1979).

- **Cultivate anchoring and group cohesion.** Build further on
the "anchors" and group cohesion you established for your
employees in the previous stage.

- **Invite risk taking.** Encourage direct reports to try new
things—to take some risks. Ask "What could we do about this
particular problem?" Each risk that succeeds will build confidence and prepare people for the final stage.

Stage Four: Acceptance and Adaptation

Most employees will eventually accept their new situation and adapt
to it. Others may drift off to new jobs they find more satisfactory—

either inside or outside the organization. A certain number will never adapt, however, and their performance will suffer. Here are some things you recommend to managers for helping themselves and their direct reports through this final stage:

- **Keep working on group dynamics.** Remember that people are generally less concerned with the tasks they are given than how they fit in with the group.

- **Understand what each employee needs to feel a sense of accomplishment.** For one person, that might be an opportunity to demonstrate her special talent for creating PowerPoint presentations. For another, it could be his project management ability. For each person, find that special talent and give the individual an opportunity to use it and to earn some recognition.

- **Move the focus from feelings to action.** Action will take employees' minds off their hurt feelings and insecurity, which will eventually fade away.

- **Be prepared to "outplace" individuals who cannot or will not fit into the new situation.** These individuals will be a permanent drag on performance and cast a negative pall over the unit.

The advice given here about listening, accepting, and supporting may seem overly simple and obvious. But it's these simple and obvious actions that managers often overlook. Don't make the same mistake. (For an inspirational story on how one leader managed change under stressful circumstances, see "How Shackleton Did It.")

Stress-Management Training

Employee training provided by HR can also help people manage workplace-related stress. The most effective stress-management training programs have the following characteristics:[3]

- **They provide information.** The facts about stress must be made clear. These include (1) the biochemical manifestations

How Shackleton Did It

Thanks to many books and films produced over the past few years, most readers are probably familiar with the ill-fated Antarctic expedition of Sir Ernest Shackleton and his ship, *Endurance*. Though he utterly failed to accomplish his intended goal, Shackleton's success in holding his crew together, and in returning all to safety, has made him quite a hero. Managers of all stripes can learn much from his management and leadership in that period of extreme adversity.

The *Endurance* left England in 1914 with the goal of landing on the Antarctic shore and sending a team of men and dogs to the other side of the continent by way of the Pole—a feat that had not yet been accomplished. But Shackleton never made it to the staging area. Trapped by an ice pack in the Weddell Sea and unable to move, ship and crew were forced to stay put for almost fifteen months until the ice broke up. How Shackleton held his team together and kept them alive in the world's most inhospitable environment provides insights into change management.

Like employees in a change situation over which they had no control, the *Endurance* crew saw that the goal they had enlisted for was abandoned. Everything they had hoped for and had prepared for had to be scratched. They were out of communication with the world they knew and could expect neither help nor rescue from any quarter. When the pressure of the ice eventually crushed the sides of the ship, slow starvation or death from exposure became highly probable.

In April 1916, the ice floe on which the crew had survived for more than a year began to break apart. Lifeboats crammed with men and supplies were launched into the frigid sea—the first leg of a long and harrowing journey toward safety. And despite months of continued hardship and peril, every member of the Shackleton expedition survived and—together—returned safely to England.

Continued

How did their leader keep the expedition's members from mentally and physically shutting down under these circumstances? Here are three actions taken by Shackleton that proved effective:

- **He immediately provided a new and acceptable goal.** The crew would live on the ice pack until it broke up; they would then navigate to safety via the ship's lifeboats. As long as people had a worthy goal to work toward, their energies and spirits were maintained.

- **He kept everyone busy.** Fifteen months on an ice floe could have driven the crew to fratricide. So Shackleton made sure that everyone kept busy. Meteorological data was recorded daily. Regular soccer matches and dogsled races between teams supported group cohesion and maintained mental and physical health. A drama group was created to perform theatrical entertainment. Until the ship was eventually crushed, crew-members tended to necessary repairs. A core team planned for the eventual voyage by lifeboat. Holidays were celebrated.

- **Difficult and undesirable chores were equally shared.** Shackleton, the ship's captain, and other leaders lived and worked with everyone else. There was no sense of "them" and "us." They were in it together.

of stress (the flooding of the hormones adrenaline and cortisol into our system), (2) the harmful impact of these chemical responses (headaches, fatigue, anxiety, muscle tension, insomnia, depression, and even stroke, hypertension, and heart problems), and (3) the costs associated with stress (decreased productivity and morale owing to irritability, fuzzy thinking, and declining creativity). When employees learn about stress's dangers, they have more incentive to change how they respond to stress triggers.

- **They provide techniques that employees can use on the job.** These techniques include deep-breathing exercises, guided imagery, and music therapy. Additional techniques include listening to relaxing music or concentrating on positive imagery while driving to work during rush hour.

- **They emphasize "performance enhancement" over "stress management."** Some people worry that taking a "stress course" indicates that they're overly sensitive or emotional, or that they have some sort of mental problem. To avoid activating this stigma, "market" your stress-management program as a performance-enhancement training. Require it for all employees, and make sure people see it as essential to business success.

- **Their results are tracked.** As stress-management training programs are ongoing, track business outcomes in the form of productivity, absenteeism, turnover, and other "vital signs" of the business.

Channeling "Good" Stress into Positive Results

In addition to helping managers ease their employees through the four stages of adapting to stress and providing effective stress-management training, you can show managers how to channel the adrenaline generated by stressful times into "good" rather than "bad" stress—and turn "good" stress into positive results. "Bad" stress has distinctive symptoms—including employees' unwillingness to commit to deadlines, consistently missed targets, an aversion to risk-taking, and unwillingness to volunteer even for high-profile opportunities. "Good" stress—indicated by a drive for continuous improvement at individual, departmental, and corporate levels—is the kind you want managers throughout your organization to foster and channel toward change.

How can managers channel good stress in the right direction? Show them how to establish a system of performance-based rewards and punishments that they consistently and equitably administer. As Peg Gamse, director of corporate resources at RS Information Systems in Virginia, explains:

When employees achieve stretch goals or make significant headway toward achieving them, . . . recognize the results and the people that attained the results publicly with financial or nonfinancial rewards that are important to staff. When employees fail, . . . let them know promptly and in private that they have done so.[4]

Gamse offers additional recommendations: Coach employees who have failed, and "provide them with additional, appropriate resources." Then "monitor the situation closely. If particular employees continue to fail, . . . reassign the employees—not for punitive reasons—to jobs at which they are more likely to succeed, . . . withhold monetary increases or, as a last resort, . . . fire the poor performers."

According to Gamse, to transform bad stress into good stress and productive action, managers need to:

- Be ready, willing, and able to assemble pertinent data and plans of action

- Create, communicate, and carry with them "hip-pocket" plans that address changing business needs in a variety of circumstances

- Model measured risk-taking

- Demonstrate leadership by communicating goals as well as the steps to achieve them—the "who, when, how, and at what cost" details

- Clearly define the expectations of success

- Make midcourse adjustments based on performance, progress toward goals, and ability to achieve desired outcomes

- Evaluate performance of people, products, and process before defining the next set of expectations

Rethinking Resisters

Although we addressed the issue of change resistance in a previous chapter, it's important to reexamine it here. That's because such resistance is a natural human response—one with which all managers must learn to cope.

"Resister" typically describes anyone who refuses to accept the change, or who doesn't change as quickly as do others in the same situation. Many managers view resisters as obstacles to be overcome. They see them as people with poor attitudes, or as lacking in team spirit. But treating resisters this way only intensifies real resistance, thereby thwarting or at least sidetracking the possibility of change. Your role, as an HR professional, is to help managers develop a different way of treating resistance.

How? Remind managers that resistance is part of the natural process of adaptation to change—a normal response from those who have a strong interest in maintaining the current state and guarding themselves against loss. "Why should I give up what has created meaning for me?" they ask. "What do I get in its place?"

Also explain that resistance is generally more complicated than "I won't." It involves a much more painful question: "Why should I?" Once managers understand resistance as a natural reaction— part of a process—they can view it more objectively as a step in the process that leads to acceptance and adaptation. At the very minimum, resistance denotes energy—which managers can work with and redirect toward positive ends. The strength of resistance, moreover, indicates the degree to which change has touched on something valuable to individual employees or the overall organization. By helping managers discover what that valuable something is, you can help them guide themselves and their employees through the change effort more effectively. One theorist puts it this way:

> First, [the resisters] are the ones most apt to perceive and point out real threats, if such exist, to the well-being of the system, which may be the unanticipated consequences of projected changes. Second, they are especially apt to react against any change that might reduce the integrity of the system. Third, they are sensitive to any indication that those seeking change fail to understand or identify with the core values of the system they seek to influence.[5]

Thus, resisters may provide important information. Managers who dismiss them as naysayers may be making a serious error. Instead, encourage managers to rethink resistance to change by trying to see it as something most of us human beings do to protect ourselves. Resistance provides a potential source of energy, as well as valuable information about the change effort and direction. Your advice to managers throughout your firm? "Rather than viewing all resistance as an obstacle, seek to understand its sources, motives, and potentially affirmative core. You'll open up new possibilities for realizing change."

How HR Professionals Can Cope with Change-Related Stress

Your ability to help other managers aid themselves and their employees in adapting to change hinges on your own ability to cope with change. If you let *yourself* burn out, you can't help others survive a change initiative—and thrive in the aftermath. But HR managers—like all other managers—face unique stress triggers. Table 8-1 shows the more common triggers and ways to overcome them.

"HR in Action: Helping Employees Face Change" recounts one company's strategies for helping employees cope with change.

TABLE 8-1

HR Stress Triggers and Coping Strategies

HR's Stress Triggers	Coping Strategies
Bearing bad news, such as layoffs or benefit cutbacks	• Build positive relationships with all employees, so people find it easier to absorb painful news. • Understand the business rationale behind a layoff or cutback—and don't personalize the fact that you have to lay people off. • If you lose officemates to a layoff, keep your perspective. Remind yourself that many individuals go on to find satisfying work after being laid off.

HR's Stress Triggers	Coping Strategies
Balancing human and business concerns, and not being able to help employees as much as you'd like	• Honestly acknowledge that you may not be able to fix all of an employee's problems but that you're there to listen if he or she needs to talk. • Have realistic expectations of yourself. Don't chastise yourself for something beyond your control. But do try to strike a balance between being people-oriented and business-oriented. For example, if you're very people-oriented, work on looking at situations from an objective business perspective as well. • Keep your goals and responsibilities as an HR professional in mind. Remember that your ultimate aim is to make the best use of your organization's human resources for the good of the overall company.
Doing more with fewer resources	• Plan for the unplanned by leaving a chunk of your day open for the inevitable crises and interruptions. • Prioritize: Know which tasks *must* be done today—and which can wait until tomorrow. • Ask for help if you need it. • Designate a block of time as interruption free—by closing your door, turning off the ringer on your phone, etc. Swap desks with an agreeable co-worker if his or her workspace offers more privacy.
Dealing with information overload	• Take time to clarify your priorities and to set aside information that doesn't directly relate to your top priorities. • Monitor your thought patterns, replacing self-defeating, paralyzing thoughts (such as "I can't do this!") with positive ones ("This is hard, but I'll get it eventually").
Dealing with perpetually negative people	• Construct a psychic buffer zone—an imaginary cocoon into which other people's negativity can't enter, and your energy can't leak out. • Shift perpetually negative employees' responsibility for their problems back to them. For example, say something like, "That's an important problem, and I'm sure you know the answer to it." Then invite the person to come back to you when he or she has a workable solution.
Keeping personal or sensitive information private	• Find someone you can talk to about your feelings without breaking confidentiality. Clarify the reasons that you can't reveal the specifics of the situation. • Build a support system outside the organization by networking with former colleagues or joining professional associations.

SOURCE: Linda Wasmer Andrews. "Avoiding HR Burnout." *HR Magazine,* July 2003.

HR in Action:
Helping Employees Face Change

Agilent, a Hewlett-Packard spinoff, was in trouble. A general economic downturn, along with the downfall of telecoms that bought Agilent's products, had hammered at the company's revenues for several long years. Top managers knew Agilent had to slash costs to survive—but how?

CEO Ned Barnholt drew on the HP Way—the set of principles for treating employees that founders Bill Hewlett and Dave Packard had handed down—to lay out an action plan. His strategy? Cut expenses and then, if necessary, cut salaries. He asked all employees to cut discretionary spending, letting them decide which costs to trim. Without specific guidelines, they cut as much as possible—achieving huge savings.

Through e-mails, twice-weekly newsletter articles, and regular news and brainstorming meetings between managers and their direct reports, managers communicated why the cuts were necessary and how savings would help. Using the company-wide public-address system, Barnholt urged employees to keep fighting.

When cost-cutting and a temporary 10 percent across-the-board salary cut weren't enough, Agilent had to cut staff. Barnholt set the tone by announcing the news companywide before releasing the information to Wall Street—employees would hear it from him, not the news media, first. He thanked everyone for what they had done so far, then explained the company's deteriorating performance. He told listeners that downsizing was unavoidable—explaining how many people would lose jobs, where that number came from, and how the process would work. In an exhausted voice, he acknowledged that this was the toughest decision of his career but that he had used up all the alternatives.

Agilent trained 3,000 managers on the right way to let people go, then tasked them with delivering the news to the affected direct reports themselves. Managers were asked to be as honest as possible with employees, to field every question asked, and to post on the company intranet the criteria by which specific positions were eliminated, so employees could view the reasons for the decisions.

By taking steps to help people through the stages of change, communicating empathy and respect, and treating people fairly, Agilent sustained the feeling of family that permeated its workforce—during and after the downsizing. Even employees who lost their jobs gave Agilent their loyalty and devotion as long as they could. One woman worked long hours in the three weeks after she was told she'd be laid off. Rather than feeling bitter about her situation, she said, "I felt horrible that [my bosses] had to do this." And she did what she could to ease life for her coworkers who survived the layoff: "This was my gift to them: to leave my job in the best way possible."

SOURCE: Daniel Roth. "How to Cut Pay, Lay Off 8,000 People, and Still Have Workers Who Love You." *Fortune*, January 22, 2002.

Summing Up

This chapter described how people typically react to change and how HR managers can effectively deal with negative reactions. Here are some key points to remember:

- People faced with dramatic change generally respond through four stages: shock, defensive retreat, acknowledgment, and acceptance and adaptation. These stages are similar to the grieving process that follows the loss of a friend or family member. Your challenge as a change leader or facilitator is to patiently help people through these stages.

- Individuals can overcome some of the emotional problems associated with change by: regaining a sense of personal control over other areas of their lives; gaining greater objectivity of their situations by making an inventory of personal losses and gains; and "re-anchoring" themselves.

- HR managers can help people through the four stages using a number of methods, which include listening, keeping people as connected as possible to their work groups or other routines, and eventually moving them from a focus on personal emotions to a focus on productive activities. HR professionals can also provide stress-management training and can take steps to manage their own responses to the unique stress triggers they face in their jobs.

Leveraging Chapter Insights: Critical Questions

- Think about the way things are in your organization right now. Would you describe the energy as "bad" stress or "good" stress? How might you transform bad stress into good stress— and then channel that energy toward productive ends?

- If you're leading or facilitating a change effort now, what are you currently doing to help employees go through the four stages? What could you be doing better to manage the process?

- If your department offers stress-management training programs, how effective are they? Do they convey the facts about stress, provide techniques employees can use on the job, and emphasize performance management over stress management? Are you tracking the results of the programs in terms of business outcomes?

- What stress triggers do you feel most susceptible to as an HR professional? What are you doing to cope with your responses to those triggers? Are there more effective coping strategies you might use? If so, what are they?

CHAPTER NINE

Toward Continuous Change

Staying Competitive Through Change

Key Topics Covered in This Chapter

- *An explanation of continuous incremental change and its advantages*

- *How to determine whether people can handle continuous change*

- *Tips for implementing continuous incremental change in your workplace*

MANY PEOPLE erroneously believe that change and change management must always be one time events: A company, having operated under "business as usual" for many years, suddenly throws the cards in the air, everyone gets involved in reform, and then it's over. We call this "discontinuous change"—a single, abrupt shift from the past. With this kind of change, the momentum of the organization shifts, ideally to a higher level of performance or in a more promising direction.

But the benefits of a successful single fix don't last forever. Change initiatives that accomplish stated goals often lead to complacency in senior management. Units that developed market-beating products and services during the change gradually shift their attention from innovation to defending their turf. Employees settle back into routines and once again become inward looking. But with each passing day, the competitive environment and technology keep transforming. This combination of complacency, defensive behavior, routines, inward focus, and ever-evolving business realities is the enemy of progress; ultimately, it creates a situation in which major reform is needed once again.

As an HR professional, you can play a vital role in ensuring that your organization stays ahead of the change curve—not only in the way you lead change initiatives of your own, but also in the way you help other executives and managers facilitate change.

Continuous Incremental Change

To stay ahead of the pack, companies must do more than just launch occasional, one-shot change initiatives. They must create conditions in which people *continually* sense and respond to shifts in the business environment. In such organizations, managers and employees remain attuned to signals of change from customers, markets, competitors, and technologists. And they respond in appropriate ways. Simultaneously, they monitor internal activities to spot opportunities to continuously improve key processes. They communicate openly to ensure that new ideas are heard and objectively evaluated. Change is ongoing and takes place through many small steps—that is, it's continuous and incremental. Figure 9-1 graphically depicts the contrast between discontinuous and continuous, incremental change.

Continuous incremental change offers numerous advantages:

- Small changes are easier to manage than large changes.

- Small changes enjoy a greater probability of success than big ones.

- With small changes, disruption is short-term and confined to small units at any given time.

- In an organization that strives for continuous incremental change, people remain in a constant state of competitiveness and change-readiness.

- Small, ongoing changes strengthen the company's ability to fine-tune its strategy—and are less costly and damaging than large-scale, crisis-related change.

Robert Schaffer, an author and management consultant, lent support for the advantages of incremental change when he wrote that "the larger the project, the greater the likelihood that the client organization lacks the requisite implementation skills, the managerial consensus, and the motivation necessary" to exploit the broad-ranging change initiative.[1]

FIGURE 9-1

Discontinuous versus Continuous Incremental Change

Discontinuous change takes place through major, widely separated initiatives. Performance gains through those steps are followed by long periods of consolidation and quiescence.

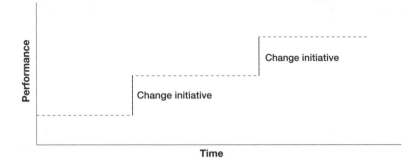

Continuous incremental change is made through a series of small but more frequent improvements.

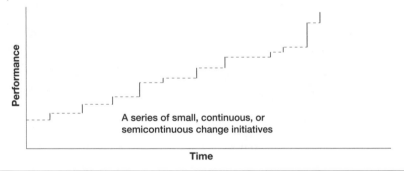

Can People Handle It?

The critical question is, can managers manage and employees function in situations of continuous change? We know that too much change is mentally and physically disabling. People need anchors and a certain level of predictability in their lives to stay mentally and physically healthy. Doctors, for example, tell us that a job loss or job change, a divorce or loss of a spouse, and a change of household address can all lead to illness and accidents. Combine two or more of these events, and you might as well keep the phone number of the local ambulance service in your pocket. In this sense, too much change is downright unhealthy.

On the other hand, few people are strangers to change in their work environments. From new technology and processes to new owners and a variety of change initiatives, change is the rule rather than the exception. The ability to adapt rapidly and frequently to new realities seems to be a critical mechanism for survival, and most people *can* handle it. This is particularly true when nonwork aspects of their lives remain stable.

We're also subject to a phenomenon called the inoculation effect. Hurricane victims, for example, exhibit a "confidence curve" as a result of repeated crisis. Individuals who have been through one hurricane are the most stressed; they become hyper-watchful and tend to overprepare when they hear the next hurricane warning. In contrast, people who have had repeated exposures to hurricanes approach impending storms with greater equanimity. They know what preparation is required, and they expect that they'll come out of the hurricane in one piece.

If this analogy is transferable, participants in continuous change may exhibit a similar learning curve. The first big change initiative may make them hypersensitive to the next one, but repeated exposures will likely inure them to change and prepare them psychologically to deal with it. However, this is only a hypothesis, and one that remains untested. And some experts speculate that the opposite could happen—that is, people exposed to repeated change could become more fragile, more resistant, and less equipped to manage successfully.

Given human differences, we might speculate that human beings' capacity to handle continuous change is tied to expectations. In some companies, people are routinely moved in and out of projects and positions; it's just how things are done in these organizations. But employees understand this from the beginning and expect constant change. Indeed, some people are attracted to certain companies precisely *because* they're fast-changing. If people know at the outset that frequent change—in positions, responsibilities, and the like—is part of the job, we can suppose that a kind of self-selection takes place. People who enjoy that kind of experience will seek out jobs in these companies; and these companies will hire individuals who can accept and embrace frequent change.

The notion of continuous change as the ideal organizational state is fairly recent, so we can't yet know this state's long-term impact on individuals. However, broad-based experience with continuous process improvement, primarily in Asia and less so in Europe and the United States, indicates that people can handle it. In Japan, people treat continuous improvement as routine!

People should be able to handle regular change as long as managers present it appropriately. Specifically:

- **Explain it right.** Lay out the reasons that ongoing change is important. Describe the dangers of *not* making continuous incremental change, and the benefits that such change offers.

- **Help people anticipate it.** Start communicating about the importance of change *before* things reach a crisis point. If you wait for a crisis, employees can only react to shifts in the business environment. The shock of change is more intense and lasts longer under these conditions.

- **Present it in manageable doses.** Don't overwhelm people with change. As Eric Abrahamson maintains, that only spawns a painful cycle of initiative overload, change-related chaos, and widespread employee cynicism. The goal is to encourage sustainable, *repeatable* transformation—not widespread destruction.[2]

- **Encourage people to participate in it.** Rather than imposing change from on high, get people actively involved in developing plans for change. That way, when it's time to implement those plans, employees will feel a greater sense of ownership over them—and make a stronger commitment to a positive outcome.

- **Make it routine.** Look for every opportunity to engineer small changes—for example, make a minor process more efficient, tinker with a particular system that could be improved, and hold a weekly status meeting in a different conference room than the usual one. By constantly experiencing changes—even small ones—people may build up a greater tolerance for it.

It also seems likely that continuous incremental change stands a better chance of succeeding and is better for a workforce's overall health than the massive and disruptive change initiatives that some corporations indulge in—usually when they are in near-death situations. In fact, continuous incremental change can save organizations from the *need* to adopt massive change initiatives. And such ongoing change can produce a cadre of managers and employees who have learned from repeated experience how to plan and implement change. Thus the overall organization becomes more flexible and change-ready.

HR's Role in Driving Ongoing Change

The following sections offer some tips on how to implement continuous incremental change in your organization and ensure that the effort succeeds.

Make Your Organization and the Individuals in It Change-Ready

As you saw in chapter 3, *organizational* change-readiness stems from

- effective and respected leadership;
- appropriate reward systems; and
- an organization that is nonhierarchical and accustomed to collaborative work.

And in chapter 4, you learned that *individual* change-readiness derives from

- personal traits, such as passion, resourcefulness, and optimism; and
- individual motivation to embrace and support change.

To encourage continuous, incremental change, determine how your organization and its managers and employees measure up on these qualities. If the company falls short on any one of these factors, resist the temptation to push continuous change. Instead, first take steps to strengthen weak areas—such as improving a leadership training program, fine-tuning reward systems, and designing comprehensive communications programs to boost managers' and employees' motivation to support change.

Continuously Monitor Internal and External Realities

The primary purpose of change is to array the organization's resources in ways that optimize its ability to deal with shifting business realities. That means you and other executives and managers, along with employees, have to understand what's going on inside *and* outside your firm. Many companies now use a technique known as SWOT analysis to conduct this monitoring. Through SWOT analysis, you assess your company's:

- **Strengths**—the internal capabilities and assets your company possesses; for example, your firm may have a particularly talented research department or marketing group, or a solid accumulation of intellectual assets such as patents

- *Weaknesses*—the internal areas in which your organization is vulnerable; for instance, perhaps the company has difficulty coming up with ideas for innovative, breakthrough products, or it is suffering from high turnover among customer-relations staff, which is hurting sales

- **Opportunities**—shifts in the business landscape that may open profitable new doors for your company by building on the firm's strengths; for example, consumers are demanding products with a new technology in which your organization has expertise and proprietary knowledge assets

- *Threats*—changes in the business environment that represent dangers for your company; for instance, real-estate prices in your area are rising so high that you're finding it increasingly difficult to attract talented employees to your firm—a problem that's resulting in skills shortages in your company's workforce

By constantly assessing your company's strengths, weaknesses, opportunities, and threats, you and other managers can identify and address problems before they loom large—and seize opportunities before rival companies do. In scanning internal aspects of your business, don't forget to consider processes, workforce skills, and systems. In scanning external realities, take into account technological, societal, demographic, political, and other manifestations of change, as described in chapter 1.

Provide Meaningful Anchors

No matter how prepared people are for regular change, they still need anchors—things that provide a sense of routine, familiarity, and continuity. As noted previously, too much change is unsettling and unhealthy. But what kinds of anchors are necessary? Years ago when he wrote *Future Shock*, author/futurist Alvin Toffler encouraged his readers to keep parts of their surroundings constant—even something as mundane as the style of clothing they liked to wear. Since the gods of fashion would change those styles, he suggested buying several pair of favorite shoes and other everyday items, and putting them on the shelf. When the current pair of shoes wore out, you'd have another pair handy, even though they had long disappeared from stores. Something similar may apply in the workplace.

First and foremost, remind yourself and other executives and managers that people are social animals and that work has a powerful social dimension. So offer a wealth of ideas for how managers can keep social linkages intact even as change is ongoing. Here are some suggestions:

- **Keep healthy, functional work teams together.** In a broad-based study of U.S. workers, the Gallup Organization discovered that "having friends at work" is a key predictor of employee retention and satisfaction. Change programs that shuffle the personnel deck and isolate people from their workplace friends and acquaintances pay a big price in terms of low morale and defection. So advise managers to avoid breaking up these relationships if they cannot make a solid business case for doing so.

- **Provide opportunities for social linkages at work.** Even if managers must occasionally break up closely linked work groups, they can buffer the consequences by offering other opportunities for social interaction: a common lunchroom, a golfing league, and so forth. These bonds may replace the ones that a change program has broken elsewhere.

- **Add a social dimension to workplace gatherings.** For example, during Monday-morning staff meetings, managers could provide donuts and fruit. People always feel more social and content at gatherings featuring food.

- **Encourage people to appreciate one another.** One company developed a ritual for its quarterly off-site strategy retreats in which employees sat in a circle and took turns describing what they appreciated about the person sitting to their right.

- **Establish an atmosphere of fun.** Another organization always put out baskets of yo-yos, Koosh balls, and other toys during business meetings. People grabbed the toys and played with them, becoming more relaxed and creative together. Playfulness can serve as a powerful social bond.

A second, higher-order anchoring opportunity is found in the purpose of the enterprise itself. James Collins and Jerry Porras, coauthors of *Built to Last*, make the point that companies that enjoy enduring success have core values, core purposes, and ideologies that remain immutable over time. Nevertheless, their strategies, product lines, and operating practices are constantly adapting to a changing world. These core elements, Collins and Porras write, act as a kind of glue that holds an organization together as it grows, decentralizes, diversifies, expands globally, and develops workplace diversity.[3]

What are *your* company's core values, core purposes, and ideologies? If they are strong, they can provide the anchors that people need to stay healthy and steady in fast-changing environments. (See "Core Values and Core Purpose" for more on this topic.)

Core Values and Core Purpose

Core values are a company's essential tenets. And they can be the secure anchor that managers and employees need to stay balanced and healthy in an environment of continuous change. Consider these examples of core values:

Walt Disney
- No cynicism
- Creativity, dreams, and imagination
- Fanatical attention to consistency and detail
- Preservation and control of the Disney magic

Nordstrom
- Service to the customer above all else
- Hard work and individual productivity
- Never being satisfied
- Excellence in reputation; being part of something special

Core purpose is a company's reason for being. Here are some examples:

3M: To solve unsolved problems innovatively

Cargill: To improve the standard of living around the world

Hewlett-Packard: To make technical contributions for the advancement and welfare of humanity

McKinsey & Company: To help leading corporations and governments be more successful

SOURCE: James C. Collins and Jerry I. Porras, "Building Your Company's Vision," *Harvard Business Review* (September–October 1996): 68–69.

Wayne Brockbank and Dave Ulrich recommend additional guidelines for helping to drive continuous incremental change in your firm:[4]

- **Use "hands-on" facilitation skills to move change initiatives forward.** For example, remind managers to identify and build on small successes and to communicate the benefits of steady change for employees and the company overall.

- **Help managers use what they've learned about change to implement new change initiatives.** Suggest that managers take stock of what went well and what didn't go as well during a recent change effort. Prompt them to decide how they can apply lessons from that experience to an upcoming, new initiative.

- **Monitor the progress of change processes.** Explain the importance of putting structures in place to continually assess progress on a change effort. Examples may include weekly status meetings for a team that's implementing a change initiative, or frequent, casual hallway conversations between employees and managers in which progress is discussed and efforts are fine-tuned.

- **Encourage others to make change happen fast.** Provide statistics, business journal and magazine articles, and other communications to ensure that executives and managers throughout your company understand the importance of continuous incremental change. Share stories from other companies that have benefited from such change. "HR in Action: Fast Change at General Motors" provides a classic example of how fast change can be implemented.

- **Help others master speedy but effective decision making.** Share experts' views on fast decision making with other executives and managers. For example, in the late 1980s, Asea Brown Boveri's CEO, Percy Barnevik, formulated his "7-3 formula": It's better to make a decision quickly and be right

HR in Action: Fast Change at General Motors

For the last several years, General Motors has set out to accelerate all aspects of its business activities. GM's size and complexity pose major challenges to such an effort. To surmount those challenges, the company's HR team and CEO created the *GoFast!* initiative. This effort focuses on enhancing decision-making and -execution speed throughout the organization. To support *GoFast!*, HR designed a decision-making and -acting protocol, which it then communicated to the company.

GoFast! scored some impressive results much earlier than anyone expected. Specifically:

- Decisions that used to take months now took hours.

- Decisions that would have been revisited dozens of times in earlier years were now made during one-day meetings.

- The time required to complete annual 360-degree performance reviews shrank by 80 percent in some departments, while showing *greater* accuracy and thoroughness.

- Equipment-acquisition cycle-time decreased in some sections from 60 to 7 days.

- Time required to enroll in flex benefits dwindled by 75 percent.

- GM reversed its downward market share trend and gained market share for the first time in decades.

- The company's market capitalization topped its competitors'.

In this example, HR added value by sponsoring fast change, providing the tools to make it happen, and helping to ensure that the company stayed the course.

SOURCE: Wayne Brockbank and Dave Ulrich, *Competencies for the New HR.* (Ann Arbor, MI: University of Michigan Business School; Alexandria, VA: Society for Human Resource Management; and Scottsdale, AZ: Global Consulting Alliance, 2003), 51.

seven times out of ten than to delay while searching for the perfect solution, he told his managers.[5] Remind managers that in today's fast-changing world, none of us will ever have all the relevant information we need to make a perfectly informed decision—nor will we have adequate time. Therefore, it's essential to learn to make decisions as quickly and as wisely as possible.

- **Ensure the availability of resources that make change happen continually and quickly.** Suggest that *early* in a change process, managers define the resources they'll need to ensure the effort's success. Encourage them to devise strategies for ensuring that those resources are available when required. And remind them that resources comprise not just dollars but also information and people. For example, recommend that managers identify the individuals in their department who possess top-notch decision-making skills or other capabilities essential for continually, fast change—and that they get these individuals' buy-in early.

Summing Up

This chapter discussed two different types of change:

- Discontinuous change was described as a single, abrupt shift from the past followed by a long period of stability, after which another major change often needs to be made.

- Continuous incremental change is characterized by a series of small, discrete changes over a long period of time.

Continuous incremental change has certain advantages:

- Small changes are easier to manage, less disruptive, have a greater likelihood of success than larger ones, and can keep an organization on the cutting edge of competition.

- Repeated exposure may inure people to change and make them psychologically better prepared to deal with it.

HR professionals can move their organizations toward continuous incremental change by helping themselves and other executives and managers:

- Make their organizations change-ready

- Conduct continuous internal and external monitoring through SWOT analysis

- Provide people with meaningful anchors

In addition, HR professionals can help drive continuous incremental change by helping managers adapt learnings about change to new change initiatives, ensure the availability of needed resources, and other strategies.

Leveraging Chapter Insights: Critical Questions

- Is change in your company generally discontinuous and cataclysmic—or continuous and incremental? How might you encourage more of the latter kind of change?

- What do you consider your company's major strengths? Weaknesses? Opportunities? Threats? How might you help your company build on its strengths to take advantage of new opportunities offered by changes in the business world? How might you help the firm mitigate threats?

- What steps is your department currently taking to provide meaningful anchors that give people a sense of routine, familiarity, and continuity? How might your department strengthen this sense throughout the workforce?

CHAPTER TEN

Common Change-Management Challenges for HR Professionals

Handling Them Effectively and Successfully

Key Topics Covered in This Chapter

- *Downsizing initiatives*
- *Companywide restructurings*
- *Acquisitions and mergers*
- *Selection and assimilation of new leaders*
- *Restructuring of the HR function*
- *New approaches to key HR programs*

As an HR professional, you frequently play key roles in many different kinds of change initiatives, including everything from reductions in force and companywide restructurings to acquisitions and mergers to new approaches to compensation, benefits, and performance appraisal. In this chapter, you'll find strategies, tips, and practical "do's and don'ts" for proactively managing these kinds of change-management challenges. You'll also see examples of how other HR professionals have led or assisted in successful efforts in these areas.

Downsizing Initiatives

Sometimes companies have no choice but to lay off employees in order to survive. Downsizing is painful for everyone involved—not just the individuals who have lost their jobs. Survivors of a layoff wonder whether they'll get the "pink slip" during a subsequent round of job cuts, and many become cynical, depressed, and unproductive. The HR professionals forced to handle the complex logistics of staff cuts "stagger under the workload and feel burdened by the line of employees seeking information or just a shoulder to cry on."[1] (See "HR in Action: Helping Employees Cope with Reductions in Force" for an example of how one HR unit coped with downsizing.)

Yet by facilitating a downsizing initiative skillfully, you can help employees *and* your company experience renewal and regeneration. Equally important, you can play an integral role in ensuring

HR in Action: Helping Employees Cope with Reductions in Force

Whether you're the person being downsized, the HR professional who has to deliver the news, or the employee still standing in the aftermath, downsizing takes its toll on all involved. It's even worse when it's done incrementally; that is, in small, agonizing bits. That was exactly the situation Lynda Ford was thrown into.

In the early 1990s, the engineering firm at which she worked in HR was going through a particularly difficult period, which seemed never-ending to all involved. Almost every week, a new "layoff list" would hit the HR staffers' desks, and they would steel themselves to deliver the devastating news. The tension in the company was palpable, and as HR people walked down the corridors, employees would disappear. People were afraid that if HR wanted to talk to them, it could only mean one thing: Their employment was being immediately terminated.

With tension and anxiety at an all-time high, it was evident that HR would have to actively help employees make the transition while preserving their dignity and giving them hope for the future. A tall order, all in all. But that's exactly the stance Ford and her colleagues took. For example, they provided the following:

- **Résumé service.** Every employee was offered the services of the HR department in developing or honing his or her résumé. Each person was given fifty professionally printed copies of the final product.

- **Reference letters.** Each employee was offered a reference letter that attested to his or her skills, abilities, and contributions. The letter made it clear that the job was lost through no fault of that person.

Continued

- **Interview coaching.** Each employee was offered the opportunity to do "mock interviewing." He or she then received coaching for improving weak areas.

- **Coordination with outside services.** The HR group provided a seamless process to interface with unemployment, other Department of Labor services, and outside training programs that could benefit laid-off employees.

- **Outplacement.** HR contacted local businesses, professional groups, associations, and recruiting and staffing agencies to let them know about the highly skilled people available for hire.

- **Use of company equipment.** If employees desired, they could arrange to use company phones to make employment-related calls. If they needed copies of their résumés or other employment documents, they could obtain those as well.

- **Health and other insurance.** HR extended coverage to the last possible date and then remained in contact with laid-off employees to ensure they didn't miss important dates for COBRA coverage and conversion of other insurance. They also continued to assist employees with insurance problems after their last official employment day.

- **Employee-assistance plan.** The employees and their family members were allowed to continue to use EAP services after their last day of employment.

Presiding over layoffs is never easy. But when HR professionals handle this challenge in a way that preserves affected employees' dignity, they can protect their company's reputation, sustain survivors' loyalty, put laid-off employees in the best possible position to find new jobs, and help their companies attract talent again once economic conditions improve.

SOURCE: Lynda Ford, e-mail exchanges with author, December 25–26, 2003.

that the initiative achieves its financial and strategic objectives. Employment-law attorney Francis Coleman has identified six keys to successful handling of a reduction in force:[2]

- **Monitor the layoff's impact on protected-category employees.** In any layoff, companies risk discrimination charges and even lawsuits if dismissed employees (especially from protected classes) believe they were unfairly singled out. To reduce this risk, urge your executive team to ask whether the layoff, as planned, is likely to terminate a disproportionate number of women, minorities, or workers aged forty and older. If it is, challenge executives to defend the termination decisions on grounds of legitimate business considerations. Document the decision-making process, and ensure that your firm gets input on the planned layoff from an experienced employment attorney.

  If managers in specific departments are going to select individual employees for layoff, take steps to ensure that no improper considerations or managerial prejudices influence these decisions. How? Help managers review employees' performance evaluations and length of service, and urge managers to think in terms of eliminating *positions*, not individuals. That is, given the company's strategic objectives, which positions or types of work are no longer necessary?

- **Determine whether the layoff is subject to federal, state, and local laws that require notice to affected employees and others.** Companies that violate federal, state, and local laws about layoffs can end up paying hefty fines. To protect your firm from these, determine whether any of these laws are applicable to the proposed layoff. Federal laws include the Worker Adjustment and Retraining Notification Act (WARN), which affects large-scale layoffs. WARN contains highly specific provisions for notifying affected employees, any unions representing them, and specified government agencies and officials of the planned layoff. The law also provides several exceptions to the notice requirement; for example, if the employees in question were hired with the express understanding that the project would be temporary. To judge the ramifications of such laws for your firm's planned layoff, ensure that your company obtains advice from a seasoned employment attorney.

- **Follow all contractual obligations.** In any layoff, collective bargaining agreements made previously may provide that terminations will be based on specific criteria, such as seniority, or that affected employees will receive severance pay. To reduce the risk of violating established agreements, make sure you're familiar with these contractual obligations at your company. Failure to abide by severance-pay agreements may violate laws such as the Employee Retirement Income Security Act (ERISA).

- **Minimize negative impacts on remaining staff, and protect your company's public image.** Urge the other members of your executive team to ensure that the company provides all the help it can to departing employees—including on-site job fairs, resume-writing and outplacement services, letters of reference, referral to employee-assistance plans, and contacts at other companies in the area that may be hiring. The more supportive your company can be, the better its reputation in the community and among future job seekers. Equally crucial, helpfulness may combat bitterness and cynicism among layoff survivors. Their level of morale will play a key role in whether your company recovers from a downsizing initiative.

- **Ensure that employment termination agreements are fair, voluntary, based on full notice and disclosure, and in compliance with applicable laws.** Some firms decide to give laid-off employees severance pay or other compensation to which they're not otherwise legally entitled in exchange for a release of any claims the workers may have against the company. If your firm has made this decision, make sure your executive team knows that such releases may not be upheld if (1) it seems that they weren't voluntary entered into, (2) that the workers did not understand which rights they were giving up by signing the document, or (3) workers didn't receive valuable consideration in exchange for signing the release.

To help ensure that such releases *are* upheld, advise executives and managers to give employees something of value that they might not otherwise have been entitled to—such as extended insurance coverage or outplacement assistance—in exchange for signing the release. Managers should also give employees ample time to consider whether to sign, and to consult with legal counsel beforehand. Releases should also be written in accessible, clear language. And with releases involving employees forty years old or older, check that they comply with the federal Older Workers Benefit Protection Act (OWBPA), which contains strict guidelines about the enforceability of releases relating to potential age-discrimination claims. Again, an experienced employment attorney is a vital resource in this area.

- **Communicate the layoff decision effectively.** To further protect your firm's public image and reduce the risk of lawsuits, provide managers with guidelines for how to communicate layoff decisions to affected employees. (See "Handling Termination Interviews: Tips for Managers" for more on this.)

"Downsizing Do's and Don'ts" provides other points to consider when communicating with an employee about a layoff.

Handling Termination Interviews: Tips for Managers

To help managers throughout your company conduct termination interviews for individual employees, suggest that they use a checklist as a reminder to cover all the bases:

- Vacation due and owed

- COBRA information

- Calculation of any money owed the company

Continued

- Any tools, keys, computers, or other items issued to the employee

- Any severance due the individual

Also, managers should provide employees affected with information about the nearest unemployment office, when their health insurance will end, what information they will share with a prospective employer, if they will provide a letter of reference, how the 401(k) pension or profit sharing will be handled, and so forth. And remind them that federal and state labor laws are strict about compensation for laid-off employees.

During the termination interview, there are a number of actions managers should take:

- Explain the reason for the meeting, the reason for the decision to lay off the employee, and everything the person can expect over the subsequent weeks.

- Let the individual vent if he or she needs to, and listen patiently.

- Offer a time in the early morning or after hours during which the person can remove personal belongings from the office, to save any embarrassment he or she may feel about being laid off. But also set a time limit for goodbyes, so the process creates minimal disruption.

- Position themselves near the room's exit and have a third party at the meeting, in case the affected employee becomes agitated.

- Secure any files, computers, or other company property to which the affected employee has access. Ask a trusted manager or employee to secure these items *before* the termination interview has ended.

SOURCE: Wayne F. Cascio, *Responsible Restructuring: Creative and Profitable Alternatives to Layoffs* (Alexandria, VA: SHRM; and San Francisco, CA: Berrett-Koehler, 2002), 37.

Downsizing Do's and Don'ts

- *Do* determine whether your company must comply with the Worker Adjustment and Retraining Notification (WARN) Act. The WARN Act generally requires employers with 100 or more employees to give sixty days' advance notice of plant closings and mass layoffs.

- *Do* analyze, before finalizing decisions as to who will be laid off, whether the layoff, as planned, will affect a disproportionate number of protected-category employees—women, minorities, workers aged forty and older. If it will, make sure that the layoff decisions are based on legitimate business considerations and are not influenced by illegal discriminatory motives. And document the decision-making process.

- *Do* urge managers to conduct layoffs on a day other than Friday, to avoid giving affected employees the weekend to brood before they can start looking for another job.

- *Don't* forget to provide managers with a written version of all the information that you think they'll need to present to laid-off employees. Many employees may not remember everything a manager has said during the termination interview.

- *Don't* underestimate the power of respect and consideration for employees during a layoff. Outplacement services and other forms of assistance not only support the laid-off employees, but can go a long way toward protecting your company's public reputation and preserving morale among layoff survivors.

Companywide Restructurings

In the Knowledge Era, more and more companies are discovering that restructuring—relying on employees to provide sustained, competitive advantage—can be far more productive than treating them as costs.[3] As Wayne F. Cascio explains, instead of asking, "What's the irreducible core number of people we need to run our business?" responsible restructuring asks, "How can we change the way we do business, so that we can use the people we currently have most effectively?"

Restructuring may consist of a number of practices. And as an HR professional, you can help develop and implement these practices. See table 10-1 for examples.

By devising restructuring programs, you encourage your company to treat employees as assets to be developed through changes in business practice—not as costs to be cut through downsizing. And you can generate huge benefits for your firm. With restructuring, employees perform well, have positive attitudes, feel committed to their jobs and organizations, and perceive decisions about pay, promotions, and performance reviews as fair. They also see their coworkers as reliable and trustworthy. Equally of interest, making the most effective use of your company's human assets can boost the firm's market value—according to one study, by as much as $15,000 to $45,000 per employee.[4]

Restructuring means reinventing a business to better compete. Here are a few examples of what responsible restructuring looks like in action:

- **Cutting expenses at Charles Schwab.** Facing a 57 percent drop in commission revenues and plummeting stock values in 2001, managers at investment firm Charles Schwab decided to cut back on expenses such as catered staff lunches and travel and entertainment. Top executives agreed to pay cuts of as much as 50 percent and encouraged employees to take unused vacation and unpaid leaves of up to twenty days. In addition, "management designated certain Fridays as voluntary days off

TABLE 10-1

Restructuring Practices: What HR Can Do

Restructuring can take several forms. HR professionals can support these forms of restructuring in several ways, as suggested by the examples below.

Restructuring Practice	How HR Can Support the Practice
Skills improvement and continuous learning	• Establish companywide professional-development opportunities for managers and employees. • Encourage other executives and managers throughout the firm to find out which skills employees want and need to develop.
Information sharing	• Find out where in your organization vital information gets blocked by functional "silos." Identify those obstacles to the affected managers and work with them to establish structures (such as weekly meetings or e-mailed reports) that free up information flow.
Employee participation in designing and implementing work processes	• Conduct a survey among managers to see how much they involve their employees in generating ideas for improving the way work gets done. Explain the benefits of involving employees in this kind of effort, and provide guidelines for how managers can invite greater employee participation.
Labor-management partnerships	• Familiarize yourself thoroughly with existing relationships between organized labor and your company's management. Assess the quality of those relationships by canvassing union leaders and members, as well as managers. Identify and seize opportunities to strengthen the relationships—for example, by suggesting more effective negotiation or dialogue methodologies.
Compensation linked to employee skills and organizational performance	• Examine how well your firm's current compensation system is tied to managers' and workers' skills and performance, and suggest changes as necessary to strengthen those links. • Provide your executive team with studies or readings explicating the advantages of performance-based compensation.

without pay for employees who didn't have clients to deal with."[5] By demonstrating that they viewed employees as assets to be developed, as well as innovating radical new business concepts such as online trading, Schwab's leadership practiced responsible restructuring.

- **Redeploying at Intel.** When new technology makes some jobs obsolete, software giant Intel "provides choices to all of its employees who are performing satisfactorily. They can take advantage of self-assessment tools, career counseling, and job listings within Intel. The company also offers displaced employees opportunities for in-house training, job tryouts, even relocation to other Intel facilities."[6] A centralized system tracks and reports all such redeployment activity. Numerous Intel employees have successfully transitioned from shop floor to sales and public relations positions, or from obsolete technology divisions to high-margin centers inside the firm.

- **Trading voluntary sacrifices for company stock at Acxiom, Inc.** In 2001, executives at database-management company Acxiom asked managers and employees to take voluntary pay cuts to help the firm survive the economic downturn. Thirty-six percent of the workforce—1,973 people—agreed to a 5 percent reduction in their paychecks. They made other sacrifices as well, such as taking unpaid vacations and agreeing to shorter workweeks. In return, Acxiom offered volunteers twice the amount of company stock as the lost pay. For instance, if someone gave up $15,000 worth of salary, he or she received $30,000 in Acxiom stock. The company saved more than $24 million, didn't have to resort to layoffs, and "gained a workforce vested in the success of Acxiom."[7]

See "Restructuring Do's and Don'ts" for pointers on how HR professionals can help their organizations adapt to a restructuring.

Corporate Acquisitions and Mergers

Corporate leaders decide to acquire new firms, sell their company to an acquirer, or merge with other firms for strategic reasons; for example, to strengthen a particular capacity, generate cash, or achieve important synergies. These major change initiatives impose unique burdens on HR professionals. In particular, you have to help

Restructuring Do's and Don'ts

- *Do* carefully consider the rationale behind your firm's restructuring policies. Clarify how the policies will improve the company's ability to meet customers' expectations and needs—and communicate that rationale to other executives and managers.

- *Do* encourage managers to make their concerns about the business known to employees and to seek workers' input before making final decisions about restructuring. Employees may have insightful ideas that make layoffs unnecessary.

- *Do* carefully examine all HR systems in light of strategic or environmental changes facing the firm. Ask, "Given our situation, what training do our employees need? How many new hires do we need, and what skills should they have? How should we appraise and reward performance? What should compensation consist of, based on changes in required skills and responsibilities? How can we involve employees and unions in the restructuring process?"

- *Don't* advise your executive team to use downsizing as a first resort when economic trouble hits. Instead, urge them to consider alternative approaches to cost reduction—no matter how many of your firm's competitors are downsizing.

- *Don't* assume that merely cutting perks is a cure-all. Instead, invite managers to look for opportunities to change the way work is done throughout your firm.

- *Don't* let employees hear about management's economic concerns through the grapevine. Instead, provide regular, ongoing updates to build trust—which is crucial to successful restructuring.

SOURCE: Wayne F. Cascio, *Responsible Restructuring: Creative and Profitable Alternatives to Layoffs* (San Francisco, CA: Berrett-Koehler; and Alexandria, VA: SHRM, 2002), 100–106.

the two affected companies mesh their plans, systems, and processes. In addition, corporate M&As often mean layoffs, as the final, new entity eliminates positions made redundant by the change.

Despite their strategic intent, "fewer than 25 percent of all mergers and acquisitions attain their desired results."[8] Equally troubling, a badly handled merger or acquisition can severely damage employees' sense of well-being, team morale and productivity, and even customer satisfaction. By contrast, skillfully managed M&As can offer important new competitive benefits, rare opportunities to change a company's culture for the better, and valuable chances to reinforce new and better ways of doing business. Moreover, integrating two companies can provide the impetus for significant changes in HR:[9]

- Demonstrating HR's project management expertise—setting the stage for a strong role in the new entity

- Shifting HR resources from transactional and administrative work to strategic and consultative roles

- Redesigning HR programs to achieve business purposes, such as attracting and retaining talent for the new company

See "HR in Action: The Making of a Successful Merger" for an example of a merger that achieved these positives.

HR in Action:
The Making of a Successful Merger

As the U.S. government slashed defense spending after the end of the Cold War, defense contractors Martin Marietta and Lockheed merged to better focus on their core capabilities: aerospace technologies. HR and other managers at the new entity—Lockheed Martin—took many steps to ensure the best possible transition. For example, they announced an ambitious schedule for the merger strategy—and kept to it. They also took the opportunity to initiate "megachanges" throughout the business (such as selling nonproductive assets) that they believed would stave off future major restructuring. And they delegated decision making to the lowest level at which people could make a considered judgment—increasing managers' and employees' buy-in throughout the firm.

Managers made additional moves to leverage the new company's human assets. For instance, to bring out people's natural competitive instincts, they began grading the performance of each division, sector, and the corporation at the end of each year. Employees among the various sister organizations couldn't resist comparing the numbers year to year. Other managers also brought customers (most of them pilots and astronauts) in to speak with plant workers, to help these workers appreciate the enormous importance of their jobs. Furthermore, they reassigned offices in the new headquarters to avoid the impression that some people were more important than others. This attention to symbolism helped employees see the transition as a merger of equals. Finally, they took every opportunity to communicate an essential message: that bringing together the best practices of several distinct companies would make the new company far more competitive than either one could have been individually.

By skillfully handling a complex merger, HR and other managers at Lockheed Martin helped the newly merged company generate impressive results. Despite a downturn in defense spending, Lockheed Martin's stock price nearly doubled in the late 1990s.

SOURCE: Norman R. Augustine, "Reshaping an Industry: Lockheed Martin's Survival Story," in *Harvard Business Review on Change* (Boston: Harvard Business School Press, 1998), 159–187.

How to help increase the odds that a merger or acquisition will provide these advantages at *your* company? Start by taking care of yourself; after all, if you get overwhelmed by the possibility of the kind of transition that comes with such changes, you'll become less able to help your company navigate the move. Also, get involved in merger or acquisition discussions as early as possible—don't wait for the change to actually take place. Mitchell Lee Marks offers these guidelines:[10]

- **Seek information.** When people feel that outside forces are reducing their control over their own lives, they often try to regain a sense of control by walking out the door—or by fixating on matters beyond their power (such as the fact that the CEO hasn't shared more information about what's going on). To exert control, seek information by taking your boss to breakfast and finding out what you can about the potential acquisition or merger. But realize that with most M&As, there's no master plan, and no one has all the answers.

  If your company may be acquired, contact HR counterparts at the buyer to see what you can learn—or to provide information they may find helpful. Also get in touch with local business reporters and business school professors who have studied the acquiring company, to see what they can tell you about how the firm has handled past acquisitions. And if you're worried about losing your job, prepare a personal contingency plan, including networking possibilities, courses, or certification programs that may enhance your employability.

- **Listen to yourself.** Ask what emotions you're feeling—and whether you're controlling those feelings or they're controlling you. Many people fear expressing any sense of vulnerability during a merger or acquisition, assuming it may be used against them if there's a layoff. Others may feel excited at learning that an acquiring company is committed to something they value highly—such as a "world-class HR group." All of these feelings are normal. Find a way to identify and express them, perhaps through keeping a journal or talking with a trusted friend or counselor. Your goal? To vent negative emotions and highlight positive ones.

- **Be patient with yourself.** M&As put multiple demands on HR professionals. If something falls through the cracks (a missed deadline, less-than-perfect service to your internal customers), don't beat yourself up too much about it. Ask for a bit of flexibility on deadlines during the transition period, and prioritize the work on your plate. Embrace the learning opportunities offered by mistakes.

- **Anticipate the next transition.** Often, acquisitions and mergers set off a series of copycat combinations in an industry. To prepare yourself and your company for possible additional transitions in the future, sponsor periodic workshops that help staff learn from the current transition and master personal well-being during times of change.

"M&A Do's and Don'ts" provides useful guidelines for HR professionals to observe during an M&A restructuring.

M&A Do's and Don'ts

- *Do* protect HR credibility by taking a strategic approach; for example, by focusing on designing and implementing innovative solutions to people-related business performance issues in the new firm.

- *Do* get your own "HR house" in order before a merger deal is closed, so you can prepare HR to support implementation once it begins. For example, use third parties—such as a vendor to set up and operate a temporary call center—to plan ways of handling administrative activities that will be related to integration.

- *Do* ensure that HR services are used to best advantage during integration—by assigning HR staff to business-unit integration teams. This lets HR stay close to business issues *and* build relationships with new business-unit managers.

Continued

- *Do* attend to important roles during the first 100 days after the merger. For example, set the people-related strategy for the new organization (such as retention plans, capability requirements, and vital resources). Also, develop the senior leadership team by persuading executives to clarify roles, assign accountabilities, and agree on decision-making processes.

- *Don't* cherry-pick best practices from the two merged companies' HR organizations. Too often, this ends up in compromises and disappointment—as well as an HR function that lacks coherence. Instead, align HR policies, programs, and practices with the new company's business requirements— then design the HR function to meet those requirements effectively and efficiently.

- *Don't* ignore competitors' capabilities. Analyze gaps between your company's capabilities (such as getting products to customers on time, managing costs effectively, serving customers, etc.) and rival companies' capabilities. Identify and address causes of any gaps—whether it's *people* (insufficient staffing), *culture* (an emphasis on reacting rather than planning), *process* (lack of procedures for conducting effective workforce planning), *structure* (no assignment of responsibility for strategic staffing), or *technology* (no systems to enable efficient workforce planning).

SOURCE: Jeffrey A. Schmidt (ed.), *Making Mergers Work: The Strategic Importance of People* (Alexandria, VA: SHRM, 2002), chapter 7.

Selection and Assimilation of New Leaders

Consider these disturbing statistics:[11]

- Between 1995 and 2001, turnover among chief executives soared 53 percent.

- During that same period, CEO tenure plunged more than 23 percent, and the number of CEOs who left their jobs under pressure more than doubled.

- Two-thirds of the world's companies have changed CEOs at least once in the last five years.

What's going on? CEOs have come under enormous pressure to deliver results quickly. If they don't deliver, they're sent packing—and such failures can cost a company twenty times the executive's salary. If they do deliver, competitors may lure them away. All this puts pressure on HR professionals to help new chief executives hit the ground running and to ensure that the new leader continues meeting the organization's objectives. HR leadership is particularly crucial in the first six to twelve months of a new CEO's tenure—when the board of directors and shareholders closely evaluate his or her performance. (See "HR in Action: Enhancing Leadership Bench Strength" for an example of how these objectives have been met in one company.)

Whether it's a new CEO, a new general manager of a division, or any leaders making their way to the top of the corporate-governance ladder, HR professionals play a central role in determining how well these individuals assimilate into the company and how consistently and reliably they serve the organization's needs. Many experts have found that "the responsibility for designing and implementing [a leadership selection and assimilation strategy] typically resides in the HR department.... HR [must] act as advocate for the individual and ensure that the objectives of the organization are being met."[12]

To serve as this kind of advocate, you need to get to know new leaders, make a good first impression, and provide incoming executives with the information they need to do the job. Robert J. Grossman offers these guidelines:[13]

- **Get to know the new boss.** Find out as much as you can about an incoming leader *before* he or she starts the new job. Talk to the person's former colleagues, and read any relevant

HR in Action:
Enhancing Leadership Bench Strength

In 2001, Schwan Food Company created its own corporate university to address pressing issues, including leadership development and succession. According to Arnie Strebe, president of "Schwan's University," senior executive education courses were considered the most crucial. Strebe called in HR and other experts from around the country to develop the firm's leadership program, including defining what kind of leaders would best suit the company.

Company executives and experts eventually identified fifteen competencies they believed senior-level leaders should have—for example, "managing vision and purpose," and "developing direct reports." They then built programs to help leaders gain the experience required to develop these competencies. In addition, program developers used 360-degree feedback (assessments from an individual's supervisor, peers, and direct reports) to gauge each person's strengths and weaknesses. Resources for improvement include executive coaching, training, and a number of other approaches.

The faculty ultimately created more than four hundred individual development plans tailored to different individuals. "We can see it working in example after example," Strebe maintains. And the response to the program has been "overwhelming."

SOURCE: Christopher Cornell, "Fail Safe," *Human Resource Executive*, June 2, 2003: 33–36.

articles in the business press. Try to discern his or her attitudes toward the HR function. What kinds of HR programs were in place at the person's last company?

- **Make a good first impression.** Suggest a meeting with the incoming leader before he or she comes to town. Demonstrate your value by offering information and an open door if the person has questions. In a relaxed social setting, ask, "What's your operating style? How do you lead? How do you want to move forward in terms of strategic planning?" Then communicate the person's vision to your staff—early and often.

- **Provide valuable information.** To succeed in their role, new leaders require specific information. In your first meetings with a new CEO, for example, come prepared with details on how the company is doing with retention and filling vacancies. Who are the peak performers? What process is in place for removing mediocre performers? What are employees' concerns and issues? How does the company compare with rivals on compensation and benefits? Have data on hand demonstrating your plans for the future of the company's HR function. Offer a succession planning document, and use facts, figures, and ideas to show how you intend to make your HR operation best in class. Gather metrics—retention rates, average sale per employee, cost of goods per employee, etc.— indicating what the firm needs to do in the next year or so with its human capital in order to remain competitive.

- **Share your assessment of workforce skills.** Give new leaders your thoughts about which specific skills and capabilities your firm needs most to stay ahead of the pack. Share your assessment of how managers and employees measure up on these key capabilities, and how the organization can best strengthen weak areas.

In addition to the ideas above, improve new leaders' chances of success by developing rigorous, disciplined leadership-development programs in your firm. If your company has to keep hiring new leaders from outside, take a closer look at your internal executive-development efforts. By improving your company's leadership "bench strength," you can help ensure that the right leaders will be available from within the company—when they're needed. (See "Leadership Selection and Assimilation Do's and Don'ts" for pointers on how HR can enhance the selection and bench strength of leaders.)

Leadership Selection and Assimilation Do's and Don'ts

- *Do* shape the executive-selection process early. Identify where your organization is in its life cycle, and ask what ideal characteristics successful new leaders will need. Help selection-committee members establish criteria *before* they go out to interview candidates. Offer committee members reading materials and facts about what to look for in a leader.

- *Do* demonstrate to new leaders that you can think like a business partner. Highlight problems and issues among current reporting executives—and their likely successors—that could damage the company's overall performance.

- *Do* find out how a new leader likes to receive information. Is he or she a detail person? Does the individual prefer a general overview? If you have to, simply ask the person about his or her preferences.

- *Don't* deluge new leaders with paper and with "HR-speak" and minutiae. Have reports in hand with executive summaries, but rely more on frank discussions and oral analysis of the facts and figures. Be prepared to respond at whatever level of detail the boss requires.

- *Don't* assume that a new CEO values the HR function highly. Find out what his or her attitudes toward HR have been in the past. Take even stronger steps to establish your credibility if the person has a history of not valuing what HR professionals can bring to the table.

- *Don't* wait for incoming or rising leaders to get in touch with you before they start their new role. Make contact yourself. Invite them to dinner, and let them know that you want to get to know them better and get a read on their leadership style. Ask them what they want from you as they ease into their new job.

Restructuring of the HR Function

As today's companies face ever-stiffening competition, many are drawing more heavily on the HR function to sharpen their competitive edge. By serving as true strategic partners—rather than as administrative and transactional managers—HR professionals are helping their companies align human capital behind the corporate strategy. (See "HR in Action: Realigning the HR Function" for one company's successful experience with HR restructuring.)

HR in Action: Realigning the HR Function

In early 2000, the HR department at Wells Fargo Bank's San Francisco Bay region set out to shift its role from administrative to strategic. The transition wouldn't be easy: The department's 14 staffers served 185 branches, 3,000 employees, 5 market presidents, and 15 market-area managers. The department's new vision called for HR to serve as consultants to the region's managers—to present HR solutions that would improve the company's bottom line.

To realize its new vision, the HR group needed to restructure itself. It had been set up as a silo—with the VP of HR at the top and HR consultants and staffing managers in separate divisions, all centralized at headquarters. But now staff needed to be closer to their clients. The solution? Have HR consultants and recruiters work at the branch level as an integrated team to support managers—and move all administrative responsibilities to a centralized location at headquarters.

Rolland Kwok, vice president of HR, hired an outside consultant to help HR staffers to develop the skills and knowledge needed to serve in their new role. The consultant defined eight consultative roles for the HR team:

- **Technical expert:** giving managers information and advice

Continued

- **Coach:** asking managers questions and providing motivation and feedback that help others develop professionally

- **Process facilitator:** keeping managers focused on their unit's goal and ways to get there

- **Problem solver:** searching for clues and evaluating solutions

- **Administrator:** managing schedules, budgets, and resources

- **Influencer:** selling ideas and broadening managers' perspectives

- **Strategist:** considering the big picture and overall direction of the firm

- **Partner:** balancing results with managers' trust and commitment through collaboration

The fourteen HR staffers next received training in ways to meet with managers and find out what these internal clients needed from HR. By gathering and analyzing data, and conducting surveys and one-on-one meetings, the HR team developed and presented potential solutions to their clients.

The results of the HR restructuring proved remarkable. Employee turnover shrank 19 percent, saving the company $500,000. Centralization of administrative duties saved branch managers three hours a week—total $975,000 in savings per year. A new recruiting structure reduced the time to process new-hire paperwork from fourteen to seven days. Equally intriguing, the HR staffers felt more valued than ever and derived more satisfaction and enjoyment from their jobs.

SOURCE: Adrienne Fox, "HR Team Makes Leap to Strategic Partner," SHRM *HR News*, May 21, 2003.

But redefining HR's role from administrative to strategic often requires major changes in the HR department's structure, processes, systems, and skills—its very infrastructure. To engineer those changes, you need to take a disciplined approach. Dave Ulrich recommends the following steps:[14]

1. **Define the right architecture for the HR organization.**
   Experts recommend that to serve as strategic partners, an HR
   department's staff members need the following:
   - A shared identity as strategic partners in the firm
   - The knowledge, skills, and attitudes to perform current and
     future responsibilities related to strategy
   - A performance-management system that encourages a focus
     on supporting corporate strategy
   - Effective reporting relationships, communications, decision-
     making processes, and policies
   - The ability to learn and adapt to change
   - Sufficient leadership skills

2. **Create an assessment process.** For each of the characteristics
   listed in Step 1, rate your HR department on a scale of 1 to
   10, where 1 indicates "definitely needs improvement" and 10
   indicates "best practice." The exact numbers you use matter
   less than the discussion evoked during the assessment process.
   These ratings can be done by a task force of HR professionals
   within your firm, by external consultants or advisors, or by
   clients within the firm.

3. **Provide leadership in improvement practices.** Restructure
   HR practices to improve areas identified as weak in Step 2.
   For example, if HR staff members need to acquire particular
   competencies, decide whether you'll accomplish this through
   hiring talent from outside the organization, upgrading
   current staff members' skills and knowledge, or partnering
   with an outside consulting company to provide specific
   HR services.

4. **Set priorities.** Focus the HR function's resources on those
   few critical restructuring efforts that you believe will yield
   the biggest "bang" for every implementation "buck." That
   way, you'll get the most from resources that are often stretched
   thin during such change efforts.

   "Restructuring HR Do's and Don'ts" offers points to consider
during an HR restructuring.

Restructuring HR Do's and Don'ts

- *Do* define your goals before meeting with internal clients to discuss a new structure and role for HR. Ask yourself, "What do *I* need to accomplish at this meeting?" If you don't clarify this beforehand, the other party may take you where *they* want you to go—not where *you* need to go.

- *Do* make each interaction with internal clients a positive one. Demonstrate that you're there to find out how you can serve their needs, and stress the benefits to the bottom line promised by HR's new structure and role.

- *Don't* assume that each member of your HR team must be able to play all eight roles described in "HR in Action: Realigning the HR Function"—from technical expert to partner. The overall team must be able to play these roles at any given moment. Sometimes assembling a team in which various members cover different bases will do the trick.

- *Don't* assume that focusing more on helping others in your firm means focusing less on helping HR. Every time you apply effective new principles to the HR function itself, you boost the department's ability to improve the bottom line for the overall organization. The key is to define a strategy for HR that will enable your department to support the *company's* strategy—and then make the structural changes needed to drive the HR strategy you've defined.

New Approaches to Key HR Programs

More and more HR professionals are realizing that new approaches to key HR programs can help them better support their company's strategy. For example, a redesigned performance-appraisal and compensation system can motivate managers and employees to demonstrate the behaviors, skills, and attitudes required by a newly formulated strategy emphasizing customer service. A career-development program that focuses on matching employees' most passionate interests with job opportunities can help support a strategy that hinges on employee retention. And a radically overhauled health-benefits program that gives employees more choices can reinforce a strategy centered on cost cutting. (See "HR in Action: Implementing a Radical New Health Plan" for an example of how one HR unit introduced and effected a new health benefits program.)

HR in Action: Implementing a Radical New Health Plan

Like many other firms, trucking company J.B. Hunt was seeing employee health-insurance plan costs skyrocket in the late 1990s and early 2000s. As an antidote to a 15 percent inflation rate on costs, Hunt's HR vice president Mark Greenway decided to introduce a consumer-driven health plan (CDHP) in 2003. In CDHPs, a high-deductible PPO is coupled with an annual employer contribution to an employee health-care reimbursement account (HRA), allowing for residual funds to be rolled over from one year to the next.

Though a CDHP represented a dramatic alternative to the more traditional health-care plan offered at Hunt, it resonated with other HR initiatives at Hunt that centered on encouraging employees to be more responsible for their choices. For example, the company has a cafeteria-style benefit plan and had been moving toward a self-service model for HR administrative functions.

Greenway has worked to clarify the CDHP's desired outcomes, design the program to boost chances of generating those outcomes, and educate employees on how to use the pro-

Continued

gram. For example, he established specific goals related to number of employees enrolled in the CDHP, cost trends, and utilization rates for particular services. He also priced the CDHP so that it's somewhere between the company's HMO pricing and its PPO pricing.

Finally, he designed a comprehensive communication program to educate employees on the new plan. HR personnel first talked with employees about health costs in general and what cost increases meant to the company. Then they explained the concept and advantages of consumer-driven health plans. Only then did they convey details about the specifics of the new plan. By explaining the principles and economics before getting into the cost of the plan for employees, Greenway and his colleagues laid the groundwork for employees to understand and accept the plan.

Thanks to HR's efforts, the CDHP is showing great promise at J.B. Hunt. Though it's too soon to assess the plan's long-term impact, Greenway expects that two-thirds of the employees who signed up for the CDHP will have residual funds in their HRAs at year end. He also feels confident that almost all of the employees who chose the plan will continue to re-enroll.

SOURCE: Richard F. Stolz, "Driving Change," *Human Resource Executive*, May 2, 2003.

These sorts of change initiatives present important challenges and opportunities. Whatever program you're developing or redesigning, keep as open a mind as possible. Brainstorm plenty of alternatives, and look for ideas that offer win-win solutions for everyone concerned. The highest-leverage change efforts will be those that most strongly align behind the company's overall strategy. (See "Redesigning HR Programs Do's and Don'ts" and "Tips for Leading HR-Related Change Initiatives" for strategies for developing and implementing HR programs.)

Redesigning HR Programs Do's and Don'ts

- *Do* ensure that changes to your HR programs reflect your company's values. For example, if your firm emphasizes employee participation and responsibility, a consumer-driven health plan may reinforce those values.

- *Do* pay close attention to program design. Set up details such as pricing and choices so that the new program accomplishes the desired outcomes. Resist the urge to grab a promising-looking program out of sheer desperation.

- *Do* make a thorough and aggressive effort to communicate the changed program to employees. The more they know about the changes ahead of time, the more equipped they'll be to get the most from the program.

- *Don't* expect your new or revised program to pay big dividends forever. Business realities are always changing, and you need to be ready to make additional changes to your firm's HR programs to stay current.

- *Don't* forget to enlist support from senior management in launching a new or revised program. Executives can help get employees to informational meetings—which in turn increases the likelihood of employee buy-in.

- *Don't* expect to see financial results from a redesigned HR program immediately. These payoffs can sometimes take several years to show up.

Summing Up

In this chapter, you learned how various HR professionals in a broad range of companies and industries have led or facilitated a wide array of change initiatives that pose unique challenges for HR:

Tips for Leading HR-Related Change Initiatives

Though this chapter describes a wide array of HR-related change initiatives, HR professionals need to apply a shared set of principles to successfully manage these efforts:

- **Educate yourself.** No matter what the initiative, learn as much as you can about the bigger, strategic picture that forms the context for the change. That way, you can ensure that the initiative's outcome will support your company's strategy.

- **Take the initiative.** Don't wait around to get the information and make the contacts you need to lead the change effort. Initiate conversations with your boss, with peer managers, without outside information sources—whoever can provide the perspectives and information you need to design and implement a successful change.

- **View each initiative through the lens of strategy.** Whether you're leading a corporate restructuring, assimilating a new CEO, or orchestrating any of the other change initiatives described in this chapter, always consider how well the change effort reinforces your company's strategy.

- **Take the long view.** Anticipate potential long-term impacts of actions you're taking. For example, how might you handle a downsizing so that your company will be able to attract the talent it needs once the economy recovers?

- Downsizing

- Corporate restructuring

- Acquisitions and mergers

- Selection and assimilation of new leaders

- Restructuring of the HR function

- New approaches to HR programs

Leveraging Chapter Insights: Critical Questions

- Of all the change initiatives described in this chapter, which ones has your company experienced? How did HR contribute to designing and implementing the initiatives? What were the results?

- Which of the six change initiatives described in the chapter do you anticipate happening in your company over the next few years? What steps can you take now to prepare for these efforts?

- Of the six initiatives described in the chapter, which do you feel best prepared to lead or facilitate? Why? How might you strengthen your abilities on the remaining initiatives?

- In what ways could you restructure the HR function at your company, or design or introduce new HR programs, to better support your firm's strategy?

CHAPTER ELEVEN

HR as Change Agent

*An Unprecedented Opportunity—
and Responsibility*

Key Topics Covered in This Chapter

- *The behaviors of strategic partners in change*
- *Steps to becoming a strategic partner in change*
- *Checklist for leading a successful change initiative*

A S YOU'VE probably concluded from the preceding chapters in this book, HR professionals have an unprecedented opportunity to serve as change agents and leaders. And as the twenty-first century dawns, this shift in HR's role is becoming more crucial than ever. Executives around the world are assessing accelerating change and realizing that it's their companies' human resources—not technologies, manufacturing plants, or capital equipment—that offer the best hope of adapting to and profiting from change. And in light of the growing mistrust in corporate leadership (at least in the United States), these same executives know that, again, only *people* can restore confidence in business leaders.

HR professionals have more than just an opportunity to proactively lead change in their organizations—they have a responsibility to do so. Yet this new role requires a specific mind-set that may call for a shift in focus, and a new way of operating in your company. This concluding chapter explores these topics and describes a three-phase process for becoming and staying a strategic partner in change initiatives at *your* organization. At the end of the chapter, you'll also find a checklist that you can use as a blueprint for successfully leading or facilitating a change initiative in your company.

Strategic Partners in Action

Being a strategic partner in change starts with *seeing* yourself as a change agent.[1] According to Randall MacDonald, senior vice president of HR at IBM, too many HR professionals today "live in a cocoon . . . comfortable with the support organization."[2] To lead change, HR professionals must remind themselves that successful and enduring change hinges on managers' and employees' ability to anticipate, adapt to, and benefit from the forces constantly buffeting businesses. That means *managing* these vital human assets—with an eye specifically toward change.

What behaviors must you demonstrate if you're seeking to strengthen your abilities as a strategic-change partner and human-asset manager? Consider the following:

- **Take the initiative.** Rather than allowing yourself to be classified as an operational, legal-compliance, or administrative-support person, view yourself as a change *catalyst.* Instead of waiting for change initiatives to be delegated to you, jump-start the changes you believe are essential for your company to survive and thrive in its competitive arena.

- **Know your company.** Understand your own company. That includes learning as much as you can about your company: its strategy, its challenges, and its business model. It includes proactively walking around, listening, and learning. It requires building a network of relationships in the organization and maintaining regular contact with members of that network to stay attuned to what's going on inside the firm. It hinges on grasping the needs of external customers. And it includes grasping the needs and abilities of internal customers—the managers and employees you and your department serve.

- **Know your business.** Understand the business or industry in which your company operates. Learn as much as you can about who your competitors are, what competitive advantages—and weaknesses—your company has, what the trends in the industry are, and the challenges that the future is likely to bring. Again, use your internal network to keep up-to-date on this information. Read industry magazines and journals. Attend industry meetings and conferences.

- **Know business in general.** Educate yourself about business, whether you work in a for-profit or nonprofit world. Learn the principles, language, economics, measurements, and other tools of your type of business. Take a course in general business or nonprofit management. Keep on top of business trends by reading business periodicals and books.

- **Develop leaders.** Cultivate a pool of leadership talent that your organization can draw on now and in the future. That requires knowing what skills will most reinforce the company's competitive strategy, attracting the managers and employees who possess those skills, and providing the training and professional-development resources to cultivate future leaders. It also means understanding that the most successful companies boast alumni who run other accomplished firms. For example, people who honed their leadership abilities at one firm may go on to head businesses that constitute their former employer's customers, suppliers, and partners. Finally, developing leaders requires an ability to handle leadership transitions smoothly—for instance, leveraging the strengths of a former CEO to complement those of a new chief executive.

- **Cultivate a climate of pride, innovation, and empowerment.** Encourage others to take pride in their work, to take risks and learn from mistakes, and to have a voice in how change unfolds in the company. Know that without pride, innovation, and empowerment, managers and employees simply cannot feel a sense of ownership in major change initiatives. And without a sense of ownership on the part of people at all levels in an organization, most change efforts will fall flat.

- **Speak up.** Just as you empower others to have a voice in change, you must also have the courage and conviction to speak up decisively and candidly about what you think your company needs to successfully navigate change. Truly change-ready CEOs want HR executives and managers who are "comfortable with leading, who can focus on winning, who can execute, and who can create . . . sustained momentum. And they want people who will believe in what they're out there espousing and have a passion for it."[3]

- **Add value.** Come to work every day asking, "How can I make this process or this system better? How can I improve my company's ability to compete? Where does each unit fit in my company's strategy, and what skills to the people in those units need?" Rather than welcoming change for change's sake, look for opportunities to continually add value for your organization. That value may take several forms; for example, identifying what's next or new in the business world, or cultivating the functional excellence needed in each business unit. Value can also come in the shape of accountability throughout the workforce: Managers and employees do what they've promised to do—on time, within budget, and to the agreed-upon standards.

Where to Go from Here?

You've absorbed a lot of information while working your way through this book's chapters. How do you pull it all together and begin applying your new knowledge in the workplace? If your company is like most, there are likely numerous change initiatives either in the works or in the conceptualization stages. These give you plenty of opportunities to put your deepened understanding of change management into practice. David E. Ripley, author of several SHRM white papers, recommends a three-phase approach to preparing yourself to lead or facilitate a change initiative: (1) conduct a strategic HR analysis, (2) align HR to the business, and (3) prepare for change. Together, these three phases enable you to clarify the "big picture" of a change initiative—and HR's role in it—before you jump into leading or facilitating the effort. Let's take a closer look at each phase below.

Phase 1: Conduct a Strategic HR Analysis

In conducting a strategic HR analysis, you and other executives engage in the following steps:[4]

1. **Define your company's** *strategic intent.* Strategic intent is the picture of where and what company leaders want the organization to be in the future. If your executive team hasn't already defined the firm's strategic intent, encourage the other members to explore questions such as:
   - "Who are we, and what are we trying to accomplish?"
   - "What business are we in, and what is our purpose as an organization?"
   - "What do we want to be in the future?"
   - "How do we add value in the marketplace?"

   If you think that the firm's strategic intent isn't clear, have your department conduct a survey assessing employees' understanding of company strategy—and report the results to the executive team. If you can demonstrate that workers cannot articulate the corporate strategy, you stand a better chance of convincing the rest of the executive team that they need to clarify and communicate that intent more vigorously.

2. **Develop alternative future scenarios.** *Future scenarios* are the possible situations your company might face if certain factors that exert a major impact on the business—such as raw materials costs, interests rates, and so forth—changed drastically. There's a wealth of information and case studies available on how to do "scenario planning." For example, Royal Dutch/ Shell's efforts in this area, and the results the company gained, have attracted widespread attention. Research this practice, and offer your executive team articles, books, or case studies demonstrating scenario planning's power.

3. **Define the company's strategic positioning.** *Strategic positioning* describes (in broad terms) how your company will deal with the future scenarios the executive team has defined, should those scenarios come to pass. Through strategic positioning, a company decides how it will distinguish itself from rivals so as to remain competitive in a shifting business climate. For example, will the firm explore alternative sources of supply? Enter new markets? Beef up production and manufacturing?

Again, by sharing examples of how other companies have defined their strategic positioning, you can help spark discussion about this subject among other executive team members. One excellent resource is Michael E. Porter's "What Is Strategy?" article, published in the February 2000 issue of *Harvard Business Review*, which provides numerous examples of how companies have set out to distinguish themselves from competitors.

4. **Determine key HR issues.** *Key HR issues* are questions raised by the organization's strategic intent and positioning. Issues related to *strategic intent* tend to be "big picture"; for example, "Does our company have the skills it needs to accomplish our strategic goals?" "Are our structures and processes appropriate for our desired future?" "Should we outsource functions or processes that aren't part of our core business?" Issues related to *strategic positioning* tend to be more specific; for instance, "For each future scenario we developed, what is the appropriate mix of permanent staff, contingent staff, and outsourcing?" "For scenarios that call for significant growth, what skills do we now have available in our workforce for stimulating that growth?"

Together with the rest of the executive team, brainstorm the key HR issues raised by the strategic intent and positioning the team has articulated. Explore possible answers to these questions. You'll play a vital role during these discussions, so you'll need to draw on the full extent of your strategic knowledge.

Phase 2: Align HR to the Business

Once you and other executives and managers have defined your company's strategic intent and strategic positioning, you engage in *business planning*.[5] A business plan provides a road map to achieving the firm's strategic intent and positioning. It lays out specific operational goals and objectives that each function in the company must meet to support the company's strategy. HR planning is a subset of business planning, and consists of these steps:

1. **Determine the HR contributions needed to achieve business goals.** Identify the staffing resources required to accomplish the objectives laid out in the various units' business plans.

2. **Decide which processes and activities to retain and which to outsource.** Ask yourself, "Which functions are we not performing well enough to achieve our plan's goals? Can we get somebody who performs these functions better to do them for us at a cost we can live with?" "Should we explore alternatives to outsourcing? For example, might we offer employees who are currently handling a poorly performing function the opportunity to form their own company and bid on the work? Should we provide better training to improve the function's performance?"

3. **Align current HR programs and policies with business-plan objectives.** Examine each existing HR program to see if it's truly required to accomplish the objectives on the business plan. If a program is not needed to meet objectives, ask, "Is it *legally* required?" and "Does it reflect our company's values?" If you answer "No" to both questions, seriously consider eliminating or realigning the program. Also consider which new HR programs you might need to establish in order to meet the business plan's objectives.

4. **Develop action plans for realignment, elimination, or establishment of HR programs.** Once you've decided which HR programs to realign, eliminate, or establish, develop action plans to implement these changes. In each plan, specify which objective the plan is designed to accomplish, which activities the plan comprises, which individuals or teams will take responsibility for implementing the plan, what schedule the plan's implementation will follow, and what metrics you'll use to evaluate the plan's performance.

Phase 3: Prepare for Change

Now that you've helped clarify your company's strategic intent and positioning and have aligned HR to the business plan, take steps to prepare yourself and your company for continuous change.[6]

1. **Define new concepts and values as anchors.** To be continually ready for change, managers and employees must stop thinking of their organization in terms of established procedures and processes and instead envision it in terms of new concepts and values. These serve as "anchors." Examples of new *concepts* might include "We must embrace change" and "We must empower the workforce." Examples of new *values* might include "Our company helps people develop the skills they need to manage their own careers." Use questionnaires and focus groups to determine what concepts and values employees think are most important and most accurately define the company. Refine the concepts and values until they reflect what's needed for the company to prepare itself for change.

2. **Define new boundaries.** Replace "authoritarian" boundaries (rigid reporting hierarchies) with "authority" boundaries—protocols specifying who's in charge of what, who's responsible for accomplishing which tasks, what's in it for people who fulfill their responsibilities, and who constitutes members of which teams. Ensure that each authority boundary meets three criteria: It is porous (it improves communication and information flow); it is clear enough to guide individuals and teams as they adapt to change; and it has been established with employees' input.

3. **Make structures and processes congruent with the new anchors and boundaries.** Decide whether current organizational structures (such as reporting arrangements) and processes (e.g., purchasing methods, order-processing approaches, etc.) align behind the newly identified anchors and boundaries. Use employee focus groups to get answers to questions such as, "If one of our anchor concepts is empowerment, do team members have to struggle through several layers of supervision to take needed actions? If so, how empowered are they, really?" Or, "If we've defined a boundary that gives a team responsibility for purchasing routine supplies, does the team actually have the authority to make these purchases?"

4. **Make the company's culture congruent with the new anchors and boundaries.** Unlike structures and processes, organizational culture is hard to define and document. Often, people in a company simply understand the firm's culture in terms of how people act, what values they stand for, what they can count on in the organization, and which behaviors are considered acceptable. Once executives have defined the company's strategic intent, they'll find it relatively easy to determine the values, philosophies, beliefs, and practices needed to support that intent. But this doesn't mean that the company's *actual* culture matches this *desired* culture. Again, use employee surveys and focus groups to see how closely your firm's real culture reflects the needed culture. Ask questions such as "What do we *really* do, versus what we *say* we should do?" Identify gaps between desired and actual culture and the changes needed to close them.

5. **Make HR policies and programs congruent with the new anchors and boundaries.** Just as you align structures, processes, and culture behind the stated new anchors and boundaries, you need to align HR policies and programs. Examine each policy and program, asking yourself how strongly it reinforces the company's stated new direction. If you've carefully worked through Phase 1 (conducting a strategic analysis) and Phase 2 (aligning HR behind the business), you've already tested HR policies and programs against strategic and business goals from an operational perspective. Further review against newly defined anchors and boundaries should prove relatively straightforward.

Checklist for Leading a Successful Change Initiative

To begin pulling together the information you've gathered from this book and applying it to your own situation, see assessment tool 11-1.

Assessment Tool 11-1 *Worksheet for Leading a Successful Change Effort*

Use this worksheet as a blueprint for leading or facilitating a change initiative in your organization.

The "Big Picture" *(see chapters 1 and 11)*

1. What is your organization's strategic intent and positioning?

2. Which new concepts, values, and cultural characteristics would best enable your firm to fulfill its strategic intent?

3. Which external forces of change might exert the most impact on your company's ability to achieve its strategic intent?

4. What possible future scenarios can you envision that might result from those forces?

5. What change initiatives might be needed to deal with those future scenarios?

6. Are your company's HR programs aligned in a way that will enable your firm to successfully implement those change initiatives? If not, which programs need realigning? Which need to be eliminated? Which new programs need to be established?

7. What new authority boundaries must be put in place to support the change initiative?

8. How well do your company's structures and processes support the new concepts, values, cultural characteristics, and boundaries you've defined? What changes, if any, might be needed to improve alignment?

Continued

Organizational and Individual Change-Readiness
(see chapters 2, 3, and 4)

9. What might you do to help establish a pool of respected and effective leaders in your company?

10. What reward systems might best encourage organizationwide change-readiness?

11. How might you replace rigid organizational hierarchies with communication and authority systems that better support employee participation in and commitment to change?

12. What steps might you take to challenge complacency, give people a voice, and drive out fear associated with change?

Eight Steps to Change *(see chapter 5)*

13. How will you establish a sense of urgency for implementing the change initiative you've identified earlier?

14. How will you create a guiding coalition to drive the change effort? Who should participate in the coalition? Why?

15. What might be a compelling vision for the change initiative?

16. How will you communicate the vision?

17. How will you empower others to act on the vision?

18. What short-term wins might you plan for and create to generate and sustain momentum for the change initiative?

19. How will you consolidate these short-term gains and use them to produce still more change?

20. How will you help anchor new approaches, new ways of doing business, in your company's culture—so that these new ways become "business as usual"?

Developing a Change-Implementation Plan
(see chapter 6)

21. Whose support and involvement do you need to develop a plan for implementing the change initiative you've identified? How will you obtain that support and involvement?

22. Which behaviors do you need to demonstrate, and which messages do you need to send, in order to support your implementation plan?

23. Which enabling structures should you put in place to support implementation?

24. How will you help people focus on the desired results of the change initiative?

25. How will you celebrate milestones once the implementation plan is rolled into action?

26. How will you communicate about the change initiative during its implementation?

Helping Employees Adapt to Change
(see chapters 7, 8, and 9)

27. Who are the change resisters and change agents in your firm?

28. How will you deal with those people who are most likely to resist the change initiative you've identified?

29. How will you leverage change agents' energy to carry out the initiative?

30. How will you help people move through the four stages of coping with change: shock, defensive retreat, acknowledgment, and acceptance and adaptation?

Continued

31. How will you help *yourself* manage the stress associated with change?

32. In what ways might you encourage continuous, incremental change—rather than overwhelming, cataclysmic change—through the initiative you've identified?

Special Change-Management Challenges
(see chapter 10)

33. Do you anticipate seeing a major change effort handed down by your company's senior leadership that will present special challenges for HR? For example, is there a companywide restructuring, an acquisition or merger, or a downsizing in the works? If so, how can you best meet the unique challenges posed by such an initiative?

34. In order to serve as a strategic partner in change for your company, does the firm's HR function need to be restructured? If so, how? And what can you do to ensure the most successful restructuring possible?

35. What changes to HR programs would better enable your company to achieve its strategic intent? For example, does your firm need a new approach to compensation, benefits, career development, promotions, or performance appraisal to compete more effectively in the business world? If so, in what ways might you alter these HR programs?

Summing Up

This chapter described the opportunity that HR professionals now have to serve as strategic partners in change for their organizations. It showed the behaviors that characterize what strategic partners and change agents look like in action:

- Taking initiative

- Understanding the business

- Developing leaders

- Cultivating an environment of pride, innovation, and empowerment

- Speaking up

- Adding value

The chapter also laid out a three-phase process for preparing to lead or facilitate change in your organization:

Phase 1: conduct a strategic HR analysis

Phase 2: align HR behind the business

Phase 3: prepare for change

Finally, the chapter provided a worksheet to use as a blueprint for leading or facilitating a change initiative in your organization.

Leveraging Chapter Insights: Critical Questions

- Think of a change initiative that's imminent for your organization, or that you believe should be launched to improve your firm's competitiveness. What areas do you need to work on most (e.g., understanding your company's competitive strategy, seeing how HR might be aligned to support the strategy, and so forth) to best position yourself to lead or facilitate this change effort? How will you work on those areas?

- What change-management areas do you consider your strongest? How might you leverage those strengths to lead or facilitate successful change in your firm?

Implementation Tools

This appendix contains four forms that you may find useful at various times as you're leading or facilitating a change initiative. All are adapted from Harvard ManageMentor®, an online help source for subscribers. Here's a list of the forms found in this appendix:

1. **Assessment Tool A-1: How Effective Are You as a Leader?** Use this form to evaluate your own leadership capabilities. Change programs require leadership at all levels.

2. **Assessment Tool A-2: Manage Stress.** This checklist helps you identify and manage stress in yourself and others during a change initiative.

3. **Assessment Tool A-3: Keep People Focused.** This checklist helps you identify obstacles encountered in the change process. Use this form to keep managers and employees focused on the most important problems during a change initiative. For each obstacle, list and evaluate options for overcoming it. Also list any allies, additional resources, or special training people in your organization will need to collaborate most effectively on the chosen option.

4. **Assessment Tool A-4: Gather and Share Information.** This checklist helps you master the all-important business of communicating during a change initiative. Use this form to collect and summarize the information managers and employees need to receive in order to support and embrace the change initiative.

Assessment Tool A-1
How Effective Are You as a Leader?

The questions below relate to characteristics of effective leaders. Use the questions to evaluate whether you possess these characteristics. Use the results to see where you might focus to strengthen your leadership skills.

Characteristics of Effective Leaders

Caring

1. Do you empathize with other people's needs, concerns, and goals?

   Yes   No

2. Would staff members confirm that you show such empathy?

   Yes   No

Comfort with ambiguity

3. Are you willing to take calculated risks?

   Yes   No

4. Are you comfortable with a certain level of disruption and conflict?

   Yes   No

Persistent, tenacious

5. When pursuing a goal, do you maintain a positive, focused attitude despite obstacles?

   Yes   No

Excellent communicators

6. Do you listen closely (rather than have a response ready before the other person finishes)?

Yes No

7. Are you comfortable running meetings?

Yes No

8. Are you comfortable making presentations and speaking in public?

Yes No

9. Do you have the skills needed to negotiate in a variety of settings?

Yes No

Politically astute

10. Could you diagram for yourself your organization's power structure?

Yes No

11. Can you articulate the concerns of your organization's most powerful groups?

Yes No

12. Can you identify those individuals within your organization who will support you when needed?

Yes No

13. Do you know where to turn for the resources you need?

Yes No

Continued

Able to use humor

14. Do you know how to use humor to relieve tense or uncomfortable situations?

   Yes   No

Levelheaded

15. In situations that are full of turmoil and confusion, do you stay calm and levelheaded?

   Yes   No

Self-aware

16. Are you aware/can you describe how your own patterns of behavior impact others?

   Yes   No

If you answered "yes" to most of these questions, you have the characteristics of an effective leader.

If you answered "no" to some or many of these questions, you may want to consider how you can further develop these effective leadership characteristics.

SOURCE: HMM Leading and Motivating.

Assessment Tool A-2
Manage Stress

What bothers the individuals in your organization the most about the current changes in your workplace? What are the sources of the stress?

How can you minimize or eliminate the excess stress?
_____ Give advance warning, minimize surprises.
_____ Encourage information sharing.
_____ Foster a sense of humor in the workplace.
_____ Reassess/reassign work tasks to balance workloads.
_____ Recognize feelings and encourage people to express them.

What sources of support (including peer or supervisory support) can you enlist to help manage stress levels?

List the names of people in your company who are exhibiting the most noticeable signs of stress. What are each person's prevailing emotions right now? Identify ways in which you can respond to each individual.

Name	Symptoms	Ways to Respond

SOURCE: HMM Capitalizing on Change.

Assessment Tool A-3
Keep People Focused

Obstacle to Implementing the Change Initiative	Options for Overcoming the Obstacle	Rank the Options (1 = most promising 5 = least promising)	Allies, Resources, Special Training

SOURCE: HMM Capitalizing on Change.

Assessment Tool A-4
Gather and Share Information

When was the last time you updated people in your organization about the latest developments in the current change process? What were managers' and employees' specific concerns?

List the most significant new initiatives currently under way for the company as a whole—for specific individual units or for the HR function.

What are the major rumors about change now running through the organization? What information about each rumor can you share with people in the company?

Continued

How can you make information about the change and about
rumors most effective? For example, should you use one-
on-one meetings? A general meeting held once a month?
A companywide memo issued weekly? An article in the
company newsletter? A combination of all of these?

Development/Rumor/Initiative	Communication Channel	Timing

SOURCE: HMM Capitalizing on Change.

Choosing Change-Management Consultants and Outplacement Firms

The management consulting business—which includes services that specialize in change management—has grown to be a multibillion-dollar business, and it continues to expand. As a group—and despite a number of notable and controversial failures—consultants have much to offer. The problem for HR professionals is discerning when to hire one or more consultants to serve as change facilitators, whom to hire, and how to work with them successfully. What types of change initiatives are best suited to outside consultants? How do you choose the most compatible consultant or firm? What level of service should you expect? And what are the keys to managing the relationship? This appendix can help you answer these questions. The information herein is adapted from Tom Rodenhauser's article in *Harvard Management Update,* "How to Choose—and Work with—Consultants" (September 1998); Thomas J. Ucko's book *Selecting and Working with Consultants* (Crisp Publications, 1990); and online articles about outplacement services from Lee Hecht Harrison's Web site, www.lhh.com.

Choosing Consultants

When to Hire a Consultant

Generally, there are two reasons for hiring a consulting firm to help manage a change initiative: (1) the change effort focuses on new processes, technologies, systems, or knowledge for which the company lacks the internal expertise; (2) your firm is considering a strategic business change—for example, expanding into new geographic areas—that requires outside, objective counsel. Consultants are, first and foremost, advisers. But their advice is no substitute for certain preliminary work that only you (or your company) can carry out. So, before considering hiring a consultant, ask yourself four questions:

1. **Do you understand the change initiative's objective clearly?** Clients and consultants often have different views of a change project's ultimate goal, and these objectives are often vaguely defined (for example, "improve a business process"). A consulting assignment without measurable targets usually results in disappointment. Before contacting consultants, spell out the scope and purpose of the proposed effort.

2. **Does management fully support the use of consultants—organizationally and financially?** Lack of support from senior management can guarantee failure of any attempt to bring in a consultant. All too often, frontline managers advocate consulting services without the full support of higher-ups. Conversely, senior executives may foist their favorite consultants on HR and other managers. The resulting internal disconnect wastes time and money and breeds distrust, which can poison the change initiative. Reach consensus with senior management on the need for outside counsel before going forward.

3. **When should the engagement end?** Consulting assignments should have a definite beginning and end. Your ultimate goal is to help managers and employees in your organization move from depending on consultants to supporting, implementing, and sustaining change themselves.

4. **Can your company provide the necessary ongoing support after the consulting engagement has ended?** Consulting is like exercise: without dedicated follow-up, it's wasted effort. To ensure continued success, monitor managers and employees

closely after the consulting engagement has ended. Assess whether people are applying what they've learned from the consultants and embedding their new knowledge in their everyday work.

Finding the Right Consultant

This is a daunting task for those unfamiliar with the industry. Some database and directory companies, such as Dun & Bradstreet and Gale Research, identify more than 200,000 U.S. consulting firms. An equal number can be found in Europe and Asia. These sources can help you pinpoint consulting firms by the industries they serve, their geographic location, or the services they provide. Most large consultancies have offices in every major city and are thus easy to contact. Increasingly, smaller firms are advertising their services via Web sites or through such brokering services as The Expert Marketplace or the Management Consultant Network. You can also search for potential consultants at industry association meetings and conferences and in trade journal or industry magazine articles. Don't forget to ask colleagues for referrals as well.

First develop a list of candidates, using the following process:

1. **Decide the type of consultant you want.** Do you want someone who'll primarily provide information in the form of written research reports? Someone who provides advice and recommendations? Someone who implements new systems or programs, and who acts as temporary staff? Someone who uses coaching and team building to help people in the company do something better themselves?

2. **Define the ideal consultant.** Specify the characteristics of the ideal consultant. For example, what kind of experience, industry background, and personal traits should he or she have? Should the person be local? Do you need one person or a team of consultants? What can you pay for the engagement? Do you prefer a person or company that charges a fixed project fee or a daily or hourly rate?

3. **Interview candidates.** Invite promising candidates in for an interview. Ask questions such as "What is your understanding of our needs?" "How would you approach this project?" "How does your approach differ from other change-management consultants?" "What can you tell me about similar engagements you've done—both successes and failures?" "What kind of information will you need to gather for this engagement? How would you acquire it?" During the interview, be sure to listen at least 70 percent of the time. (You can't learn while you're talking.) And ask open-ended questions ("how," "when," "what," etc.), rather than questions that prompt a yes or no answer. Draw out the candidate's limitations, and find out not only *what* the person accomplished during similar engagements, but *how*.

4. **Evaluate the candidates.** Compare your impressions from each interview with your list of criteria developed in Step 2. Which candidates seem best suited to the engagement? Also consider other factors, such as your sense of the candidates' trustworthiness, interest in the project, concern for you and your organization, and integrity.

5. **Check references.** Ask candidates for the names of two or three clients for whom they've done similar work. Then call those clients and ask them questions such as "How did you like working with this consultant?" "How would you describe the project he/she handled for you?" "What methods, techniques, or solutions did the person/firm offer?" "What results did you get?" "What are the person's/firm's strengths and weaknesses?" "Would you use this person/firm again for a similar project?"

6. **Request written proposals.** Once you've identified several promising candidates, request proposals from them. Consider proposals as the consultant's calling card. Never pay for a proposal or agree to a "handshake deal" for consulting services. And although there is no set formula for preparing a written proposal, a well-crafted document will clearly and concisely answer the following questions:

- Does the consultant understand the change initiative we want to implement?
- Are the approach and methodology for managing this change clearly and succinctly presented?
- Are the benefits quantifiable?
- What are the consulting team's qualifications and experience?
- What are the fees?

Studying the proposal will give you a good feel for the consulting firm's fit with your company. Jargon-filled proposals that don't define the end product are useless; you need to clearly understand what results the firm plans to deliver and by when.

Consultants rarely describe the specifics of their work to outsiders for fear of breaching client confidentiality. This makes in-depth reference checking difficult—but it is vital nonetheless. Ask finalists for the names and numbers of clients whose change-management engagements most closely match your own.

A Note About Fees

Many change-management consulting services are billed on a per-diem basis; retainers are used for long-term projects. The fees may seem exorbitant at first, but good consulting is worth the price—particularly when it generates clearly defined results. Establishing clear measures for anticipated results takes time. But it's a vital step, because the process itself allows you and the consultant to establish performance standards. It also helps you to attach a dollar value to the benefits, while the consultant knows what he or she will receive for the work involved.

Selecting an Outplacement Firm

In addition to selecting a change-management consultant, many HR professionals also hire outplacement firms during downsizing initiatives. High-quality outplacement services benefit displaced employees in numerous ways, including clarifying future career goals, building and updating skills, providing a job-search base and sense of support, and conveying knowledge about the job market and contacts with potential new employers. Such services benefit your company as well, by helping to maintain the morale and productivity of remaining employees, protecting the company's reputation in the labor market, and reducing the potential for lawsuits or EEO actions.

To select the right outplacement firm, consider these guidelines:

- **Assess business-related factors of each outplacement firm you're considering.** For example, how will your company's account be managed and staffed? Can the outplacement firm demonstrate a history, with references, of doing this kind of work for other organizations similar to yours in size or complexity? Can the firm provide appropriate services to all affected employees, at multiple sites if needed? What technology-based services does the firm offer? Does the firm guarantee its performance, and does it have a quality performance-measurement system incorporating feedback from client companies, laid-off workers, and the firm's own staff?

- **Assess the quality of each outplacement service you're considering purchasing.** For example, for each service, do the materials contain clear instructions for how laid-off workers can succeed in their job search? Does the service offer appropriate search planning and management tools? What is the quality and accessibility of online and print materials provided by the service? How well does the service build on adult-learning principles? Do the service's materials strike a tone and demonstrate a level of rigor appropriate for the group of displaced employees who will be using it?

Be sure to subject potential outplacement firms to the same level of scrutiny during the selection process as you do while choosing a change-management consultant. Ask for references, demand detailed information about candidates' strengths and weaknesses, and clarify desired results—and how they'll be measured—before signing a contract.

Notes

Introduction

1. Leslie A. Weatherly, "HR Executive Insights into HR Practices and Education: A Survey with Surprising Results," SHRM research paper, March 2003.

2. Dave Ulrich, *Human Resource Champions: The Next Agenda for Adding Value and Delivering Results.* (Boston: Harvard Business School Press, 1997), 31.

3. Ibid., 46–47.

4. Ibid., 184–187.

Chapter 1

1. Wayne Brockbank and Dave Ulrich, *Competencies for the New HR* (Alexandria, VA: SHRM and Ann Arbor, MI: University of Michigan Business School, 2003), 9–17.

2. John P. Kotter, *Leading Change* (Boston: Harvard Business School Press, 1996), 171.

3. Brockbank and Ulrich, 47–62.

4. David E. Ripley, "Business/HR Alignment," SHRM white paper, November 1996, and "Strategic HR Analysis," SHRM white paper, November 1996.

5. Cris Hagen, "The Role of Human Resources in Whole Systems Change: HR as Scout, Chess Master, Cartographer, and Architect," September 15, 2003, <http://www.linkageinc.com/newsletter/archives/od/role_hr_hagen.shtml>: (*link&learn Newsletter*) (accessed November 19, 2003).

Chapter 2

1. J. Stewart Black and Hal B. Gregersen, *Leading Strategic Change: Breaking Through the Brain Barrier* (Upper Saddle River, NJ: Financial Times Prentice-Hall, 2003), 177–186.

2. Michael Beer and Nitin Nohria, "Cracking the Code of Change," *Harvard Business Review* (May–June 2000): 133–141.

3. American Management Association, "1993 Survey on Downsizing" (New York: American Management Association, 1993), 3.

4. Wayne F. Cascio, *Responsible Restructuring: Creative and Profitable Alternatives to Layoffs* (San Francisco: Berrett-Koehler, 2002), 23.

5. Beer and Nohria, "Cracking the Code of Change," 134–135.

6. Dave Ulrich, *Human Resource Champions* (Boston: Harvard Business School Press, 1996), 153.

Chapter 3

1. Beth Axelrod, Helen Handfield-Jones, and Ed Michaels, "A New Game for C Players," *Harvard Business Review* (January 2002): 83.

2. Claudio Fernández-Aráoz, "Hiring Without Firing," HBR OnPoint Enhanced Edition (November 2000).

3. Edward E. Lawler III, "Pay System Change: Lag, Lead, or Both?" in *Breaking the Code of Change*, eds. Michael Beer and Nitin Nohria (Boston: Harvard Business School Press, 2000), 323–336.

Chapter 4

1. Robert Kriegel and David Brandt, *Sacred Cows Make the Best Burgers: Developing Change-Ready People and Organizations* (New York: Warner Books, 1996), 275–285.

2. Richard Luecke, *Scuttle Your Ships Before Advancing* (New York: Oxford University Press, 1994), 73.

3. For a fascinating account of GM's slow awakening to its quality problems, see Gregory H. Watson, *Strategic Benchmarking* (New York: John Wiley & Sons, Inc., 1993), 129–143.

4. Michael Beer, "Leading Change," Class note 9-488-037 (Boston: Harvard Business School, 1988, revised 1991), 2.

5. Richard Axelrod, "Democratic Approaches to Change Make a Big Difference in Turbulent Times," *Harvard Management Update*, November 2001, 3.

6. Gregory H. Watson, *Strategic Benchmarking* (New York: John Wiley & Sons, Inc., 1993), 131.

7. John L. Bennett, "Change Happens: Help Your Employees Accept It—and Adapt," *Managing Smart* (winter 2002).

Chapter 5

1. Michael Beer and Nitin Nohria, "Cracking the Code of Change," *Harvard Business Review* (May–June 2000): 133–141.

2. "How to Get Aboard a Major Change Effort: An Interview with John Kotter," *Harvard Management Update*, September 1996.

3. John P. Kotter, "Leading Change: Why Transformation Efforts Fail," *Harvard Business Review* (March–April 1995): 59–67.

4. Adapted from *Realizing Change*, an interactive CD-ROM based on the change literature of John Kotter (Boston: Harvard Business School Publishing, 1997).

5. John P. Kotter, *Leading Change* (Boston: Harvard Business School Press, 1996), 78.

6. The SQA story is told in David Bovet and Joseph Martha, *Value Nets* (New York: John Wiley & Sons, Inc., 2000), 169–182.

Chapter 6

1. Larry Alexander, "Successfully Implementing Strategic Decisions," *Long Range Planning* 18, no. 3 (1985): 91–97.

2. Michael L. Tushman and Charles A. O'Reilly III, *Winning through Innovation* (Boston: Harvard Business School Press, 1997), 190.

3. This section leans heavily on Todd Jick, "Implementing Change," Class note 9-491-114 (Boston: Harvard Business School, 1991).

4. Adapted from Rebecca Saunders, "Communicating Change," *Harvard Management Communication Letter* (August 1999).

5. Robert L. Guenther, "Is It Time to Replace Your Replacement-Planning Strategy?" *Harvard Management Update* (April 2004): 1, 2.

6. Robert H. Schaffer and Harvey A. Thomson, "Successful Change Programs Begin with Results," in *Harvard Business Review on Change* (Boston: Harvard Business School Press), 189–213.

7. Michael Beer and Nitin Nohria, "Cracking the Code of Change," *Harvard Business Review* (May–June 2000): 137.

Chapter 7

1. Eric Hoffer, *The Ordeal of Change* (Cutchogue, NY: Buccaneer Books, 1976), 3.

2. See the Myers-Briggs Type Indicator®, Consulting Psychologists Press, Inc.

3. See W. Christopher Musselwhite and Robyn Ingram, *Change Style Indicator* (Greensboro, NC: The Discovery Learning Press, 1999).

4. Ibid., 4.

5. Paul Strebel, "Why Do Employees Resist Change?" in *Harvard Business Review on Change* (Boston: Harvard Business School Press), 139–157.

6. Paul R. Lawrence, "How to Deal with Resistance to Change," *Harvard Business Review* (January–February 1969): 4–12, 166–176.

7. Robert Kegan and Lisa Laskow Lahey, "The Real Reason People Won't Change," *Harvard Business Review* (November 2001): 84–92.

8. Everett M. Rogers, *Diffusion of Innovation*, 3rd ed. (New York: The Free Press, 1983), 315–316.

Chapter 8

1. Harry Woodward and Steve Bucholz, *Aftershock* (New York: John Wiley & Sons, Inc., 1987).

2. Adapted from Todd D. Jick, "Note on the Recipients of Change," Note 9-491-039 (Boston: Harvard Business School, 1990, revised 1996).

3. Kathryn Tyler, "Cut the Stress," *HR Magazine* (May 2003).

4. Peg Gamse, "Stress for Success," *HR Magazine* (July 2003).

5. Ken Hultmans, *The Path of Least Resistance* (Austin, TX: Learning Concepts, 1979).

Chapter 9

1. Robert Schaffer, "Rapid-Cycle Successes versus the Titanics," in *Breaking the Code of Change,* eds. Michael Beer and Nitin Nohria (Boston: Harvard Business School Press, 2000), 362.

2. Eric Abrahamson, *Change Without Pain: How Managers Can Overcome Initiative Overload, Organizational Chaos, and Employee Burnout* (Boston: Harvard Business School Press, 2004), 1–7.

3. James C. Collins and Jerry I. Porras, "Building Your Company's Vision," *Harvard Business Review* (September–October 1996): 66.

4. Wayne Brockbank and Dave Ulrich, *Competencies for the New HR* (Alexandria, VA: SHRM and Ann Arbor, MI: University of Michigan Business School, 2003), 51–53.

5. Edward Prewitt, "Fast-Cycle Decision Making," *Harvard Management Update* (August 1998).

Chapter 10

1. Mitchell Lee Marks, "Surviving MADness," *HR Magazine* (June 2003).

2. Francis T. Coleman, *Ending the Employment Relationship Without Ending Up in Court* (Alexandria, VA: Society for Human Resource Management, 2001), Chapter 8.

3. This section draws extensively from Wayne F. Cascio, *Responsible Restructuring: Creative and Profitable Alternatives to Layoffs* (Alexandria, VA: SHRM and San Francisco, CA: Berrett-Koehler, 2002).

4. Ibid, 41.

5. Ibid., 50.

6. Ibid., 60.

7. Ibid., 62–63.

8. Ibid., 63.

9. Jeffrey A. Schmidt (ed.), *Making Mergers Work: The Strategic Importance of People* (Alexandria, VA: SHRM and Towers Perrin, 2002), Chapter 7.

10. Marks, "Surviving MADness."

11. Robert J. Grossman, "Forging a Partnership," *HR Magazine* (April 2003).

12. Diane Downey, with Tom March and Adena Berkman, *Assimilating New Leaders: The Key to Executive Retention* (New York: AMACOM, 2001), 5.

13. Grossman, "Forging a Partnership."

14. Dave Ulrich, *Human Resource Champions* (Boston: Harvard Business School Press, 1997), 212–228.

Chapter 11

1. This section draws extensively from Kristen B. Frasch's article "Ripe for Change," *Human Resources Executive*, September 2002, 60-65, which is based on Frasch's interview with Randall MacDonald, senior vice president of HR at IBM.

2. Ibid.

3. Ibid.

4. David E. Ripley, "Strategic HR Analysis," SHRM white paper, November 1996.

5. David E. Ripley, "Business/HR Alignment," SHRM white paper, November 1996.

6. David E. Ripley, "Preparing for Change," SHRM white paper, November 1996.

For Further Reading

Communication Issues

Larkin, T. J., and Sandar Larkin. "Reaching and Changing Frontline Employees." *Harvard Business Review* (May–June 1996): 95–104. Planning a major change in your organization? If so, chances are you have arranged a huge rally, rousing speeches, videos, and special editions of the company paper. Stop. This sort of communication does not work. If you want people to change the way they do their jobs, you must change the way you communicate with them. Drawing on their own research and the research of other communication experts from the past two decades, the authors argue that senior managers—and most communication consultants—have refused to hear what frontline workers have been trying to tell them: When you need to communicate a major change, spend most of your time, money, and effort on frontline supervisors.

General Issues

Abrahamson, Eric. *Change Without Pain: How Managers Can Overcome Initiative Overload, Organizational Chaos, and Employee Burnout.* Boston: Harvard Business School Press, 2004. Abrahamson maintains that companies must "change how they change" to avoid the cynicism, chaos, and burnout that can stymie even the best-thought-out change initiatives. Rather than obliterating everything and starting anew, Abrahamson urges organizations to reconfigure the people, structures, culture, processes, and networks they already possess. The payoff? Smoother, more cost-efficient, and less painful transformation.

Beer, Michael, Russell A. Eisenstat, and Bert Spector. *The Critical Path to Corporate Renewal.* Boston: Harvard Business School Press, 1990. Based on a study of six large corporations that tried to transform themselves, this book explains why some enjoyed greater success than others, and offers a practical approach that managers can adopt. Also worth reading

from these same authors is, "Why Change Programs Don't Produce
Change," *Harvard Business Review* (November–December 1990): 7–12.

Brenneman, Greg. "Right Away and All at Once: How We Saved Continental." *Harvard Business Review* (September–October 1998): 162–179.
Not many corporatewide change programs succeed. This one did, and
it makes for interesting inspiring reading. In 1994, Continental Airlines was headed for a crash landing—quickly running out of customers and cash. A simple strategy, executed fast, right away, and all at
once, says Greg Brenneman, president and COO of the company,
pulled it out of its death spiral. He describes the five lessons he learned
during this dramatic turnaround. With Gordon Bethune, Continental's chairman and CEO, Brenneman devised the Go Forward Plan, a
straightforward strategy focused on four key elements: understanding
the market, increasing revenues, improving the product, and transforming the corporate culture. Brenneman admits that the plan wasn't
complicated—it was pure common sense. The tough part was getting
it done. "Do it now!" became the rallying cry of the movement, and the
power of momentum carried Continental to success.

Brockbank, Wayne and Dave Ulrich. *Competencies for the New HR*.
Alexandria, VA: SHRM; Ann Arbor, MI: Michigan Business School;
and Scottsdale, AZ: Global Consulting Alliance, 2003. This book
explores the new business realities indicating the need for HR to play
a more strategic role as change agents in their organizations. The
authors describe the new competencies HR professionals need in
today's world of relentless, accelerating change, and the book contains
a wealth of worksheets, checklists, and other tools that help you to
apply your knowledge.

Kotter, John P. *Leading Change*. Boston: Harvard Business School Press,
1996. Emphasizing the need for leadership to make change happen—
and stick—this book identifies an eight-step process that every organization must go through in order to achieve change goals. It shows
where and how people often derail the process, and how those errors
can be avoided.

Kotter, John P. *The Heart of Change: Real-Life Stories of How People Change
Their Organizations*. Boston: Harvard Business School Press, 2002. This
book follows up on Kotter's *Leading Change*, providing compelling stories from people who have managed change in all kinds of organizations. Framed around Kotter's eight-step change process, the stories
reveal how the best change leaders use not just reports or analysis, but
concrete elements and demonstrations to impel people toward positive
action.

Realizing Change (part of The Interactive Manager Series of multimedia learning tools on CD-ROM). Boston: Harvard Business School Publishing, 1999. *Realizing Change,* based on John Kotter's book, *Leading Change,* is designed to help managers acquire the understanding and skills needed to lead and manage organizational change. Unlike the book, the CD version organizes the change agenda into three sequential phases: set up, roll out, and follow through. The interactive nature of the program allows users to drill down into various levels of detail on each phase, including case studies and other available readings.

Schaffer, Robert H., and Harvey A. Thomson. "Successful Change Programs Begin with Results." *Harvard Business Review* (January–February 1992): 80–89. If you think that big change programs with grandiose visions are bunk, you'll like this article. Most corporate improvement efforts have negligible results, according to these authors, because they focus on activities, not results, and there is no explicit connection between action and outcome. "Results-driven" approaches offer greater potential for improvement because they focus on achieving specific, measurable goals. By committing to incremental change, managers not only can see results faster but also determine more quickly what is working and what isn't.

Ulrich, Dave. *Human Resource Champions: The Next Agenda for Adding Value and Delivering Results.* Boston: Harvard Business School Publishing, 1997. Ulrich shows HR managers how they can collaborate to create an organization that can change, learn, move, and act faster than the competition. Ulrich urges a shift of the HR professional's mind-set from "what I do" to "what I deliver" and outlines four distinct roles essential for making the transition: strategic partner, administrative expert, employee champion, and change agent.

Leadership Issues

Black, J. Stewart, and Hal B. Gregersen. *Leading Strategic Change: Breaking Through the Brain Barrier.* Upper Saddle River, NJ: Financial Times Prentice-Hall, 2003. This book focuses on how you can help individuals become change-ready by redrawing their mental maps—the assumptions that prevent them from seeing the need for change, from changing even when they know they must, and from finishing the change after it's begun.

Conner, Daryl R. *Managing at the Speed of Change: How Resilient Managers Succeed and Prosper Where Others Fail.* New York: Villard Books, 1993. The author notes eight patterns and many principles that can be used successfully by those responsible for change in their organizations. The patterns involve the nature of change, the process of change, the roles played during change, resistance to change, commitment to change, how change affects culture, synergism, and the nature of resilience. Connor maintains that the degree to which people demonstrate resilience is the key factor in managing change successfully.

Luecke, Richard. *Scuttle Your Ships Before Advancing: And Other Lessons from History on Leadership and Change for Today's Managers*. New York: Oxford University Press, 1994. This collection of historical episodes dramatizes the plight of leaders faced with uncertainty and change. The episodes range from the Aztec world at the time of Cortez's appearance to the battle of Agincourt to revolutionary Boston. Among other features, the book contains an informative chapter on the power of ideas to drive change.

People Issues

Jeffreys, J. Shep. *Coping with Workplace Change: Dealing with Loss and Grief.* Menlo Park, CA: Crisp Publications, 1995. This short book was written for survivors of layoffs and other organizational changes, but it holds value for anyone in an organization undergoing major change.

Musselwhite, W. Christopher, and Robyn Ingram. *Change Style Indicator.* Greensboro, NC: The Discovery Learning Press, 1999. This "Study Guide" is an assessment instrument designed to measure an individual's preferred style in approaching change and addressing situations involving change. Knowing in advance how people respond to change can help you enlist their collaboration. This and Discovery Learning's other training and consulting products are available through its Web site: <http://www.discoverylearning.com>.

Pritchett, Price. *New Work Habits for a Radically Changing World*. Dallas, TX: Pritchett & Associates, 1994. This book offers guidelines for job management during radical change. The author's viewpoint is that change in organizations is only a response to change in the world, and therefore employees must take personal responsibility for their own careers.

Strebel, Paul. "Why Do Employees Resist Change?" *Harvard Business Review* (May–June 1996): 86–92. The problem with many change programs isn't the programs themselves. It's that too few people, at every level, really support the initiative with their hearts and minds. This article explains that organizations have personal compacts with their employees; change efforts fail when those compacts are ignored.

Index

Abrahamson, Eric, 164
acceptance of change, 135
  managerial role in fostering,
    147–148
acknowledgment, of change, 135
  coping with, 146–147
acquisitions. *See* mergers and
  acquisitions
Acxiom, restructuring at, 186
adaptability, and change-readiness, 51
adaptation to change, 135
  assessing capability for, 157–158
  conventional advice regarding,
    136–138
  information gathering for, 139,
    141–142
  managerial role in fostering,
    147–148
  marshaling personal resources, 140
  minimizing negative impacts of
    change, 137
  psychological aspects of, 137–143
  stages of coping, 134–135
adventurousness, and
  change–readiness, 51
Agilent, change at, 156–157
aging populations, 3
American Nonwovens Corporation,
  change implementation at, 72–73
anchoring, 147
  assessment of, 173
  providing, 167–170, 172
anticipatory change, 24
architects, of change, 11
Asea Brown Boveri (ABB), 170

assessment tools
  change agent skills, 12–13
  for change team, 95
  of change-readiness of HR, 14–17
  of corporate change philosophy,
    32–33
  of focus, 228
  of gains and losses of change,
    141–142
  of hierarchicality, 42–44
  of individual change-readiness,
    52–55
  of information flow, 229–230
  of leadership effectiveness, 224–226
  of organization's eight-step process,
    84
  of stress management, 227
  for successful change effort,
    217–220
Augustine, Norman, 189
Avery, Danny, 72–73
Axelrod, Beth, 37
Axelrod, Richard, 59

Barnevik, Percy, 170
Barnholt, Ned, 156
Beer, Michael, 26, 28, 29–30, 58–59,
  112
benchmarking, 110
Bethune, Gordon, 99, 100
Boston Consulting Group, history of,
  110
boundaries, redefining, 215
Brandt, David, 50

Brenneman, Greg, 99–100
Brockbank, Wayne, 170, 171
Built to Last (Collins and Porras), 168
bureaucracy, disadvantages of, 41
business planning, 213
  and HR plan, 214
  by HR professionals, 7–8
  steps in, 214

C performers, 37
  avoiding hiring of, 37–38
candidates for employment
  evaluation of, 39
  populating list of, 38
capabilities assessment, consultant role
  in, 111
Cargill, core purpose of, 169
cartographers of change, 11
Cascio, Wayne, 182, 184, 187
Champion International, Theory O
  change by, 29
change
  acceptance of, 63, 135, 147–148
  acknowledgment of, 135
  adaptation to, 135, 147–148
  attitudes toward, xv
  checklist for, 216–220
  consolidation of gains, 81
  continuous versus discontinuous,
    161–162
  corporate philosophy of, 32
  direction of, 88–89
  education about, 64–65
  eight-step process of, 70–90
  guiding coalition for, 76
  importance of individualized
    programs for, 88
  importance of short-term success to,
    80
  indicators of, xiii–xiv
  institutionalization of, 81–83, 107
  inventorying gains and losses of,
    139, 141–142
  loss and anxiety caused by, 133–134
  minimizing negative impacts of,
    137
  monitoring pace of, 170
  need for, xv

  nonhierarchical organization and,
    41–45
  paradoxes of, xvi
  participative work and, 45
  positive need for, 160
  preparing for, 214–216
  progress tracking and reports in,
    63–64
  reorganization caused by, 4–5
  resistance to, 64, 120–123, 128–129,
    152–154
  resource availability for, 172
  responses to, 116–129
  results-driven, 106–107
  sources of, 2–3
  stages of reaction to, 134–136
  strategic analysis of, 211–213
  stresses caused by, 132–158
  theories of, 26–34
  timing of, 24–25
  types of, 22–23
  urgency of, 71, 74–75
  vision for, 76–80
change acceleration
  by HR professionals, 6
  after September 11, 2001, 9–10
change agents, xv–xvi, 10, 129
  assessing skills of, 12–13
  behaviors of, 209–211
  characteristics of, 124–125
  identifying, 125–126
  insider-outsider as, 127–128
  types of, 10–11
change facilitation, 10
  alignment of HR in, 213–214
  change preparation in, 214–216
  phases of, 211–216
  strategic HR analysis in, 211–213
change management, 5
  attitudes in, 208–209
  business and strategic planning, 7–8
  change acceleration, 6
  culture management, 5–6, 81–83
  decision making, 6–7
  market understanding, 7
  pitfalls of, 88–89
  responsibilities of, 83–87, 209–211
change-readiness, of individuals
  assessing, 52–55, 66–67, 118–119

characteristics of, 50–51, 66
  ensuring, 165–166
  motivation for, 51, 54–57
change-readiness, of organization
  assessing, 42–45, 47–48
  barriers to, 41–44, 46–47
  ensuring, 165–166
change resistance, 128–129
  addressing, 122
  causes of, 120–121
  and change team, 96
  coping with, 64, 121–122
  described, 153
  passive, 123
  usefulness of, 153–154
  views of, 153
Change Style Indicator, 119
change team, 93–94
  contraindications for, 96
  picking, 95
Charles Schwab, restructuring at, 184
chess masters of change, 11
Cisco Systems, downsizing at, 132
cohesion, and reaction to change, 147
Coleman, Francis, 179
Collins, James, 168
communication
  with change resisters, 122
  with employees, 58, 64–65, 78–79
  graphic representation of, 100
  hiring consultants for, 85
  impartiality of, 100–101
  during implementation process,
    97–102
  of nature of change, 98
  of reason for change, 98
  repetition in, 101
  of rewards for success, 101
  of scope of change, 98, 100
  styles of, 101–102
  of success criteria, 101
  two-way nature of, 102
  of urgency, 71, 74–75
  of vision, 78–79
companywide change, overreliance
  on, 88
competencies required for leadership
  position, 38
competition, and change, 3

complacency
  assessment of, 46–47
  challenging, 57–59
ConferNow, change-readiness at, 64
confidence, and change-readiness, 51
confidence curve, 163
conservers, 118, 119
consistency, of behavior and messages,
    102–104
consultants
  for change, 31, 110
  characteristics of, 233
  choosing, 233–235
  coordinating vision with, 232
  corporate style of using, 33
  corporate support for, 232–233
  hiring of, 83
  indications for hiring, 231–232
  in implementation effort, 109–112
  managerial support for, 232
  modus operandi of, 111
  payment of, 235
  in restructuring, 197–198
  types of, 110–111
  weaning from, 111–112, 232
consumer-driven health plan
    (CDHP), 201–202
consumers, as trigger for change, 3
Continental Airlines, 57
  revitalization of, 99–100
continuous incremental change, 161
  advantages of, 161
  versus discontinuous change, 162
  evaluation of, 173
  guidelines for, 170, 172
  HR role in, 165–172
  presentation of, 164
  toleration of, 162–165
Copernicus, Nikolaus, 124
core purpose, 169
core values, 169
Cornell, Christopher, 194
cost-cutting programs, 22–23
crisis change, 24, 25
  communicating urgency for, 71,
    74–75
cultural change, 23
culture, organizational
  and change, 81–83, 210

culture, organizational *(continued)*
  importance of, 167–169
  after re-anchoring, 216
  and technical solutions, 88
culture management
  by HR professionals, 5–6
  and long-term goals, 81–83
customer-relationship management
    systems, 110
customers, as trigger for change, 3

DaimlerChrysler, 127
Darwin, Charles, 124
De Sole, Domenico, 127
defensive retreat, after change,
    134–135
  coping with, 145–146
delegation, importance of, 60
Deming, W. Edwards, 51, 54–56, 62
demographic shifts, as trigger for
    change, 3
diagnosis, consultant role in, 111
discontinuous change, 161, 162
Discovery Learning, Inc., 118–119
divestiture
  characteristics of, xiv
  leading to change, xiv
downsizing
  communication in, 181, 182, 183
  contractual agreements in, 180
  do's and don'ts for, 183
  effects of, 28, 176
  HR role in, 176–181
  keys to, 179–181
  legal issues in, 179–180
  minimizing negative effects of,
    180
  monitoring impact of, 179
  notice requirements of, 179–180
  positive aspects of, 176, 178
  termination agreements in,
    180–181
  timing of, 183
Dunlap, Al, 29, 132

economic conditions
  leading to change, xiv, 3

eight-step framework for change
  anchoring in company's culture,
    81–83
  assessment for, 84–85, 87, 89
  consolidating gains, 81
  creating a guiding coalition, 76
  communicating a vision, 78–79
  developing a compelling vision,
    76–78
  empowering others to act on a
    vision, 79–80
  establishing a sense of urgency, 71,
    74–75
  generating short-term wins, 80
  HR professionals' roles in, 83–87
  implementation of, 72–74
  origins of, 71
emotions
  acceptance of, 139
  and change-related tasks, 142–143
  coping with, 134–135
  related to mergers and acquisitions,
    190
  understanding, 138
employee retention programs, 105
employees
  adaptation to change by, 132–158
  attitudes toward change of, 78
  combating negative emotions by,
    62–65, 138–139
  coping with stress by, 148–151
  development of, 83
  dialogue with, 58–59
  downsizing of, 176–183
  empowerment of, 59–61
  focusing on change, 228
  getting feedback from, 146–147
  as idea source, 63, 65
  as information source, 58
  informing about change situation,
    58, 64–65, 78–79
  input into reward system, 40–41
  keeping teams together, 167–168
  outplacement of, 83, 106, 178
  reactions to change by, 134–136
  reassignment of, 83
  regaining control during change,
    140
  restructuring effects on, 185

role in restructuring, 185
setting standards for, 59
skills acquisition by, 65
training of, 83
as trigger for change, 3
unwritten agreements between
    company and, 133
empowerment
    to act on vision, 79–80
    barriers to, 60, 61
    of employees, 59, 61
    importance of, 210
    tips for, 60–61
enabling structures
    defined, 104
    employee retention programs, 105
    outplacement programs, 106
    pilot programs, 104
    training programs, 104–105
Enron, xiii
enterprise-linking information
    systems, 110
environmental factors, as trigger for
    change, 2–3
ethnic diversity, 3
expert consultants, 110
The Expert Marketplace, 233

failure, as trigger for change, 2
family structure, and change, 3
fear
    combating, 62–63
    guidelines for minimizing, 63–65,
        98, 100
    as motivator, 62
    paralyzing effects of, 74
Fernández-Aráoz, Claudio, 37, 38
flexibility
    of implementation plan, 97
    importance of, 61
focus
    assessment of, 33
    on change, 31
Ford, Henry, 124
Ford, Lynda, 177
Ford Motor Company, revamping in
    1970s, 56
foreign-born workers, 3

Fox, Adrienne, 198
Fuji Xerox, gap analysis by, 75
future scenarios, 8, 212
Future Shock (Toffler), 167

gains
    consolidating, 81
    evidence of, 82–83
    long-term, 82
gains and losses of change, 139
    taking stock of, 141–142
Galileo Galilei, 124
Gamse, Peg, 151, 152
gap analysis, 75
General Electric
    change at, xiii, 132
    hybrid Theory E/Theory O change
        at, 30
    training programs at, 104
    Work-Out initiative at, 30, 112
General Motors
    fast change at, 171
    J-car product of, 62
    joint venture with Toyota, 126
    malaise in 1970s, 56–57
    malaise in 1980s, 62
geopolitics, and change, 3
Gerstner, Lou, 127
globalization, as trigger for change, 3
goals
    assessing, 32
    importance of, 150
    long-term, 81–83
    short-term, 106–107
    and Theory E change, 31
    and Theory O change, 31
GoFast! initiative, 171
Greenway, Mark, 201
Grossman, Robert, 193
Grove, Andy, 128
Gucci Group, 127
guiding coalition, creating, 76

Hagen, Cris, 10
Handfield-Jones, Helen, 37
Harley-Davidson, successful change
    at, 57

health plans, consumer-driven,
201–202
Herman Miller, 82, 89, 103, 126
Hewlett, Bill, 156
Hewlett-Packard
core purpose of, 169
Theory O change by, 27
hierarchy
assessment of company level of,
43–44
characteristics of, 41
overcoming, 42, 215
problems of, 41–42, 61
Hoffer, Eric, 117
HR issues, in change, 204, 213
HR professionals
as agents of change, xv–xvi, 10–11,
208–221
analysis of competitors by, 192
business and strategic planning by,
7–8, 213–214
change acceleration by, 6
and change implementation, 72–74
change leadership by, 84
change management by, 83–87
and competitive edge, 197
consultative roles of, 197–198
and continuous incremental change,
165–172
coping with stress by, 154–157
credibility of, 191
culture management by, 5–6,
81–83
in downsizing, 176–183
as facilitators of change, 10,
191–192
and HR-related change, 204
in leadership selection and
assimilation, 192–196
market understanding of, 7
in mergers and acquisitions,
187–192
as moderators of change effects,
144–148
as motivators, 57–65
new approaches by, 200–203
project management by, 188
redefining focus of, 198–199
in restructuring, 185, 197–200

strategic analysis by, 211–213
strategic decision making by, 6–7
stress-management training by, 148,
150–151
understanding role in change,
14–17
human resource issues, of change, 8

IBM
change at, xiii, 57, 127–128
downsizing at, 132
implementation
behavioral aspects of, 102–104
celebration of milestones, 107–109
communication in, 97–102
consultants and, 109–112, 231–233
enabling structures for, 104–106
HR professionals and, 72–74
key personnel for, 93–96
planning of, 94, 97
problems in, 92–93
self-assessment for, 95, 114
summary of activities for, 113–114
implementation plan
behaviors and messages aiding,
102–104
flexibility of, 97
representativeness of, 97
simplicity of, 96
specificity of, 97
structure of, 97
information gathering and sharing,
assessment of, 229–230
Ingram, Robyn, 119
innovation, encouraging, 60
inoculation effect, 163
insider-outsider, as change agent,
127–128
insurance, during downsizing, 178,
182
Intel, 128
restructuring at, 186
interviews
coaching for, 178
termination, 181–182
inventorying effects of change, 139
emotions and, 142–143
tips for, 141–142

Japan, postwar change-readiness of, 55–56
J.B. Hunt, health program at, 201–202
J-car project (General Motors), 62
job enrichment, 40
    employee input in, 40–41

kaizen, 110
Kassel, Terry, 9–10
Kegan, Robert, 123
Kimberly-Clark, 29
Kotter, John, 5, 46, 59, 60, 95–96
    eight-step framework of, 70–90
Kriegel, Robert, 50
Kwok, Rolland, 197

Lahey, Lisa Laskow, 123
Lawler, Edward, 39
Lawrence, Paul, 123
leadership
    assessing effectiveness of, 224–226
    assimilation of, 192–196
    change by, xiv
    candidate evaluation for, 39
    candidate list for, 38
    change of, 23
    development of, 210
    effectiveness of, 36–37, 224–226
    hiring of, 38–39
    HR role in, 84–86
    information provided to, 195
    and philosophy of change, 31, 32
    pitfalls in hiring, 37–38
    pressures on, 193
    related to management, 85–87
    requirements of, 38
    selection of, 196
    training of, 83
    turnover among, 192–193
Leading Change (Kotter), 5, 46, 60, 95–96
Lee Hecht Harrison, 231
Lenin, Vladimir, 124
Lockheed Martin, formation of, 188–189
Luecke, Richard, 56
Luther, Martin, 124

Macchiavelli, Niccoló, 120
MacDonald, Randall, 208
management
    change. See change management
    and consultants, 232
    culture, 5–6, 81–83
        HR role in aiding, 83
        leadership and, 85–87
    project, 188
    of stress, 148, 150–151, 227
    succession of, 83
    training of, 83
management consulting, history of, 110
Management Consulting Network, 233
Manchester, William, 147
market understanding, of HR professionals, 7
marshaling personal resources, 140
Martin guitars, successful change at, 57
Martin Marietta, 188
Marx, Karl, 124
McDonald, James, 62
McKinsey & Company
    core purpose of, 169
    history of, 110
meetings, HR role in facilitating, 83
mergers and acquisitions
    attitudes to take during, 190–191
    benefits and pitfalls of, 188
    change caused by, xiv, 186
    do's and don'ts for, 191–192
    emotional issues in, 190
    guidelines for, 189–191
    HR role in, 187–192
    information seeking in, 190
    sample success story of, 188–189
    success rate of, 188
Merrill Lynch, changes after September 11, 2001, 9–10
Michaels, Ed, 37
micromanaging, dangers of, 60
Moore, Gordon, 128
Motorola, training programs at, 104
Musselwhite, W. Christopher, 119
Myers-Briggs personality framework, 117–118

Nohria, Nitin, 26, 28, 29–30, 112
Nordstrom, core values of, 169
Nucor, 39
NUMMI car assembly plant, 126

Older Workers Benefit Protection Act (OWBPA), 181
opportunities, analyzing, 166, 173
optimism, and change-readiness, 50
O'Reilly, Charles, 94
organization
    change-ready, 41–42, 45–47, 165–166
    complacency level of, 46–47
    core values and purpose of, 169
    culture of, 81–83, 88, 167–169
    design of, 83
    and eight-step process, 84–85
    hierarchicality of, 42–45
    nonhierarchical, 41–42
    responses to change of, 4–5
organizational learning, 110
originators, 118, 119
outplacement, 83, 178
    programs, 106, 178
    services, 178, 236
outplacement firms
    assessing, 236
    selecting, 235–236
outsourcing, of HR processes, 214

Packard, Dave, 156
Packer, Virginia, 64
participative work, and change, 45
passion, and change-readiness, 50
passive resistance, coping with, 123
performance enhancement, 151
personal compacts, 120
    dimensions of, 121
Peterson, Donald, 56
pilot programs, for change, 104
playfulness, importance of, 168
Porras, Jerry, 168
Porter, Michael, 213
powerlessness, 60, 61
    overcoming, 138–139
pragmatists, 118–119

Pritchett, Price, 78
process change, 23, 31
    assessment of, 33
process consultants, 110
process reengineering, 110
product launch
    leading to change, xiv
protected-category employees, downsizing of, 179, 183

reactive change, 24, 25
re-anchoring, 139–140, 215
    emotions and, 142–143
    tips for, 143
redesigning HR, 202
    benefits of, 200–201
    case study of, 201–202
    do's and don'ts of, 203
    after re-anchoring, 216
    steps in, 213–214
reduction in force (RIF). See downsizing
reference letters, 177
regulatory changes, 2–3
resourcefulness, and change-readiness, 50
respect
    during downsizing, 183
    factors in, 100
    importance of, 60, 168
Responsible Restructuring, 182, 187
restructuring
    do's and don'ts for, 187
    economic value of, 184
    employee role in, 185
    examples of, 184–185
    methods of, 184, 185
    reasons for, 184
restructuring of HR
    architecture for, 199
    assessment for, 199
    benefits of, 197
    case study of, 197–198
    and competitive edge, 197
    consultative roles of HR in, 197–198
    do's and don'ts for, 200
    leadership for, 199

priorities for, 199
résumés, teaching employees about,
    177
reward system, 83
  assessment of, 33
  celebration of short-term wins,
    107–109
  in change, 31, 40
  communication of, 101
  importance of, 39
  rewardable behaviors and outputs,
    39
  as part of transformational system,
    40, 105
Ripley, David, 211
risk taking
  encouraging, 146, 147
  importance of, 61
Rodenhauser, Tom, 231
Rogers, Everett, 124
Roth, Daniel, 157
Royal Dutch/Shell, scenario modeling
    by, 212

Schaffer, Robert, 106, 161
Schmidt, Jeffrey, 192
Schrempp, Jürgen, 127
Schwan Food Company, leadership
    training in, 194
Scott Paper, Theory E change by, 29,
    132
scouts, for change, 10–11
Selecting and Working with Consultants,
    231
September 11, 2001, effects of, 9–10
service excellence, 110
7-3 formula, 170, 172
Shackleton, Ernest, 149–151
shareholders, as trigger for change, 3
Shewhart, Walter, 51
shock
  caused by change, 134
  coping with, 144–145
  minimizing, 145
short-term goals, 106–107
short-term success
  celebrating, 107–109
  importance of, 80

Sigler, Andrew, 29
snake, personality type, 96
social linkages, importance of, 168
SQA furniture, 82, 89, 103–104, 126
stakeholders, as trigger for change, 3
standard setting, 59
statistical process control (SPC), 51
  American adoption of, 56–57
  Japanese adoption of, 55–56
Stolz, Richard, 202
strategic decision making, by HR
    professionals, 6–7
strategic intent, 8, 212, 213
strategic planning
  by HR professionals, 8
  and periodic strategic review, 107
strategic positioning, 8, 212
Strategic Benchmarking, 62
strategy development, consultant role
    in, 111
Strebe, Arnie, 194
Strebel, Paul, 120, 121
strengths, analyzing, 166, 173
stress
  assessing response to, 227
  change as cause of, 132–133
  coping with, by HR professionals,
    154, 155
  management of, 148, 150–151, 227
  managerial response to, 138
  positive results from, 151–152
  stages of coping with, 134–135
structural change, 22
success
  criteria for, 101
  rewards for, 101
  as trigger for change, 2
succession, providing for, 83
Sull, Donald, 127, 128
SWOT analysis, 166–167, 173

technology
  incompleteness of solutions offered
    by, 88
  innovation in, as trigger for change,
    3
  leading to change, xiv
termination interviews, 181–182

terrorism, causing change, 3
Theory E
    advantages and disadvantages of, 28
    consultant use in, 112
    features of, 26–27, 31
    goal of, 26, 33
    stress caused by, 132
Theory O
    advantages and disadvantages of, 28
    features of, 27, 31
    goal of, 27, 33–34
    and nonhierarchical organizations, 42
    personnel roles in, 112–113
Thomson, Harvey A., 106
threats, analyzing, 166–167, 173
3M, core purpose of, 169
Toffler, Alvin, 167
tolerance for ambiguity, and change-
    readiness, 51
Toyota, joint venture with General
    Motors, 126
training programs, for change,
    104–105
trust
    importance of, 61
    maintaining, 103
Tushman, Michael, 94

Ucko, Thomas, 231
Ulrich, Dave, xv, 30, 170, 171, 198
UPN-Kymmene, 29

urgency, communicating, 71, 74–75

vision
    communication of, 78–79
    development of, 76–77
    effectiveness of, 77–78
    empowerment of agents of, 79–80
    example of, 77
    long-term goals and, 82
    obstacles to, 79–80
    and short-term goals, 106–107

Walt Disney, core values of, 169
Watson, Gregory, 62
weaknesses, analyzing, 166, 173
Welch, Jack, 30, 112, 127, 132
Wells Fargo Bank, HR restructuring
    at, 197–198
Western Electric, statistical process
    control at, 51
work teams, maintaining integrity of,
    167–168
Worker Adjustment and Retraining
    Notification Act (WARN), 179,
    183

Xerox
    gap analysis by, 75
    training programs at, 104–105

About the Series Adviser

WENDY BLISS, J.D., SPHR, has experience as a human resource executive, attorney, senior editor, and professional speaker. Since 1994, she has provided human resource consulting, corporate training, and coaching services nationally through her Colorado Springs-based consulting firm, Bliss & Associates.

Ms. Bliss is the author of *Legal, Effective References: How to Give and Get Them* (Society for Human Resource Management, 2001) and was a contributor to *Human Resource Essentials* (Society for Human Resource Management, 2002). She has published numerous articles in magazines and periodicals, including *HR Magazine, Employment Management Today, HR Matters,* and the *Denver University Law Review.*

Ms. Bliss has a Juris Doctor degree from the University of Denver College of Law and has been certified as a Senior Professional in Human Resources (SPHR) by the Human Resource Certification Institute. Since 1999, she has conducted human resource certificate programs for the Society for Human Resource Management. Previously, she was an adjunct faculty member at the University of Colorado at Colorado Springs and at the University of Phoenix, where she taught graduate and undergraduate courses in human resource management, employment law, organizational behavior, and business communications. Additionally, Ms. Bliss has served on the board of directors for several professional associations and nonprofit organizations and was a President of the National Board of Governors for the Society for Human Resource Management's Consultants Forum.

National media including *ABC News, Time* magazine, the *New York Times,* the *Associated Press,* the *Washington Post, USAToday.com,* and *HR Magazine* have used Ms. Bliss as an expert source on workplace issues.

About the Subject Adviser

MIKE BEER is Cahners-Rabb Professor of Business Administration, Emeritus, Harvard Business School, and Chairman of the Center for Organizational Fitness. He is coauthor of the award-winning book, *The Critical Path to Corporate Renewal,* and his most recent book, edited with Nitin Nohria, is *Breaking the Code of Change.* Mike Beer has consulted with many Fortune 500 companies regarding organizational change. His article in the February 2004 issue of the *Harvard Business Review,* "How to Have an Honest Conversation About Your Business Strategy," articulates a new model for rapid organizational change that builds high commitment and performance.

About the Writers

LAUREN KELLER JOHNSON has contributed to several volumes in the Business Literacy for HR Professionals series. Based in Harvard, Massachusetts, Ms. Keller Johnson writes for numerous business publications, including the *Harvard Business Review* OnPoint series, *Harvard Management Update,* MIT's *Sloan Management Review,* and the *Balanced Scorecard Report.* She has ghostwritten several books and online training modules for managers. She has a master's degree in technical and professional writing from Northeastern University.

RICHARD LUECKE is the writer of several books in the Harvard Business Essentials series. Based in Salem, Massachusetts, Mr. Luecke has authored or developed over thirty books and dozens of articles on a wide range of business subjects. He has an M.B.A. from the University of St. Thomas.

About the Society for Human Resource Management

THE SOCIETY FOR HUMAN RESOURCE MANAGEMENT (SHRM) is the world's largest association devoted to human resource management. Representing more than 170,000 individual members, the Society's mission is to serve the needs of HR professionals by providing the most essential and comprehensive resources available. As an influential voice, the Society's mission is also to advance the human resource profession to ensure that HR is recognized as an essential partner in developing and executing organizational strategy. Visit SHRM Online at www.shrm.org.

Acknowledgments

The writers and advisers would like to thank the talented HR professionals and other experts who agreed to share their expertise and offer advice and stories from their experiences. They are:

Danny Avery

Dean Black

Lynda Ford

Ginny Wiley

These individuals' insights greatly strengthened the book and enabled us to provide valuable guidance to our readers.

The Results-Driven Manager

The Results-Driven Manager series collects timely articles from *Harvard Management Update* and *Harvard Management Communication Letter* to help senior to middle managers sharpen their skills, increase their effectiveness, and gain a competitive edge. Presented in a concise, accessible format to save managers valuable time, these books offer authoritative insights and techniques for improving job performance and achieving immediate results.

These books are priced at US$14.95.
Price subject to change.

Title	Product #
The Results-Driven Manager:	
Face-to-Face Communications for Clarity and Impact	3477
The Results-Driven Manager:	
Managing Yourself for the Career You Want	3469
The Results-Driven Manager:	
Presentations That Persuade and Motivate	3493
The Results-Driven Manager: **Teams That Click**	3507
The Results-Driven Manager:	
Winning Negotiations That Preserve Relationships	3485
The Results-Driven Manager: **Dealing with Difficult People**	6344
The Results-Driven Manager: **Taking Control of Your Time**	6352
The Results-Driven Manager: **Getting People on Board**	6360
The Results-Driven Manager: **Becoming an Effective Leader**	7804
The Results-Driven Manager:	
Managing Change to Reduce Resistance	7812
The Results-Driven Manager:	
Motivating People for Improved Performance	7790

How to Order

Harvard Business School Press publications are available worldwide
from your local bookseller or online retailer.
You can also call

1-800-668-6780

Our product consultants are available to help you
8:00 a.m.–6:00 p.m., Monday–Friday, Eastern Time.
Outside the U.S. and Canada, call: 617-783-7450
Please call about special discounts for quantities greater than ten.

You can order online at

www.HBSPress.org